The Book of ICON

The Book of ICON

John Herriott

John Wiley & Sons

Toronto New York Chichester Brisbane Singapore

Cover photo: Birgitte Nielsen
Designer: Tibor Kovalik

Canadian Cataloguing in Publication Data
Herriott, John
    The book of ICON

Bibliography: p.
Includes index.
ISBN 0-471-79736-7

1. ICON   (Computer).   2. Programming languages (Electronic computers).   I. Title.

QA76.8.I14H47 1985 001.64'04 C84-099770-1

The illustrations in this book were produced on the ICON using the **fged** editor and the screen dump facility. The sample graphics were drawn by Robert Sutherby and D. Michael Herriott, Grade 12 students at Brother Rice High School, St. John's, Newfoundland.

Printed and bound in Canada by John Deyell Company.
10 9 8 7 6 5 4 3 2 1

Nothing will ever be attempted if all
objections must first be overcome.
Samuel Johnson

To my wife Josephine

Contents

PREFACE

This book is about a machine, the ICON. The book will not merely explain how to use the machine but also guide you through a variety of activities designed to make you a skilled user of all the features of the ICON. In addition, you will be encouraged to explore aspects of the machine on your own — to examine the technical documentation supplied with the ICON, to make discoveries and to develop personal uses for the ICON.

The organizations and individuals who collaborated to produce the ICON included the Canadian Educational Microprocessor Corporation (CEMCORP), the firm that makes the system; the Ontario Institute for Studies in Education (OISE); the Ontario Ministry of Education; and teachers and students in selected schools throughout the province of Ontario. After training at OISE, the teachers returned to their schools and tried out the equipment with their students. The results were painstakingly monitored. The high quality of the ICON is a measure not only of the creativity and dedication of the system's designers — particularly Dr. Robert Arn — but also of the enthusiasm and co-operation of the teachers and students who tested the system.

It has a professional operating system, multi-tasking, multi-user capabilities, state-of-the-art, symbol-driven program access, hierarchical file structure, and the friendliest of user interfaces.

The limits of computer use are the limits of the imagination of the user. The user, for the purposes of this book, is anyone in any area of education, or anyone in a situation where many terminals need to connect together. Thus, for teachers, the device can be a tool aiding the planning of lessons; the delivery of lessons; the setting and marking of tests; the preparation of reports; the organization of courses; the calculation of final results; the storage and subsequent retrieval of information; the manipulation of results, information, courseware, individual lessons; and the integration of subject matter.

The ICON was three years in the designing, created by educators who dared to suggest what a product should look like and what it should be able to do in a field where such products were and are subject to almost daily change. The first thoughts appear to have been derived from experience with large main-frame computers. Certainly the ICON behaves in the same way as the large, but not-so-powerful devices of yesteryear.

For the student, it is also a tool: a means of measuring one's ability to control the outcome of a set of mental operations, the means of tapping into vast quantities of information, the means of processing that information, and of learning new facts or discovering new thoughts as a result; a means of presenting information; a means of exploration; a means of acquiring information rapidly; a means of storing new and old information; a means of passing information on to others; a means of discovering the world of organization; a means of learning about systems; and a means of self-discovery.

For the administrator at any level of education, the ICON provides all of the above, plus the assurance that all software is compatible; one machine only is required to deal with all kinds of programs that might be used, for whatever purpose, in the entire school system. This feature prevents many of the problems currently experienced in school systems where a variety of different computers running concurrently are unable to discourse with one another.

The ICON, although having been developed for the world of education, will serve just as eminently as the electronic confidante of the lawyer, the physician, the stock broker, the insurance broker, the car salesperson, the musical instrument retailer, the distributor of newspapers, magazines, books, hardware, or building supplies — in fact in any situation where power, flexibility, and ease of use are important.

This book is designed to be used while the reader is seated at the computer. It provides lots of hands-on activity. The rate of progress of the user will be an individual matter; members of a group or class should not be expected to progress at the same rate.

The book assumes no knowledge on the part of the user, yet it does not ignore the possibility that users will have had experience on machines that function differently from the ICON.

I have thought it proper to treat only those matters that pertain specifically to the ICON. Thus, the book does not teach how to program in BASIC, Pascal, or Logo, but only how to access these languages and use the editors to write such programs in them. I mention the C programming language only in passing. There is an ample supply of texts about these languages, and study of them falls properly into the domain of programming courses.

A short epilogue contains some notions on computer use in schools, notions that are entirely my own. I have sought to engender thoughts in (and perhaps some action by) all those who are concerned about and involved in education, whether as administrator, teacher, student, or parent.

Note

Although every effort has been made to ensure accuracy, it must be noted that changes are made to ICON operation from time to time. For example, when this book was first drafted, the command to format floppy disks was **rmtshell fdformat**, having been changed from **wdflopform**. Six weeks into the draft, the command had been changed yet again, to **fdformat 2**. None of these forms of that command is current!

It is likely that changes will continue to be made that will render certain commands obsolete. However, the *form* of the commands is unlikely to change. If a particular command does not seem to work, look in the relevant file (probably the one labeled ''**user_cmds**'') to find one which does.

Among the new developments in progress as this book goes to press is a new interface called AMBIENCE, which can be used instead of QNX to access files. Although a discussion of AMBIENCE is beyond the scope of this book, more information on this and other refinements of the ICON can be obtained from other sources — notably, the journal ICONOPHILE. This publication, originally developed as a newsletter for test sites, provides constant exchange of ideas and updates on the ICON, and may be obtained from CEMCORP, 1300 Bay Street, Toronto, Ontario M5K 3K8.

Trade Marks Used in This Book

The name UNIX™, used in this book, is a trademark of Bell Labs. QNX™ is a trademark of Quantum Software Systems. ICON™ is a trademark of CEMCORP, and LEXICON™ is also a trademark of CEMCORP in Canada.

ACKNOWLEDGEMENTS

A book such as this, although it is the product of one individual's labor, does not rise out of thin air. It is supported by a vast number of people, many of whom have no idea that they provided planks, struts, doors, and the necessary hardware out of which a structure might be built.

I will not list these people in any kind of hierarchical order, for none exists. I will list them as their names occur to me. In a presentation, in a meeting over a coffee, through written reviews and in giving up their time and expertise, all of these people have contributed to this book, although I alone am responsible for its final content.

These people are:

Professor R.S. (Bob) McLean of the OISE; Flavia Chow, Research Officer, OISE; Linda Harasim, Research Officer, OISE; John Morck, graduate student, OISE; John Follen, graduate student, OISE; Lorne R. Smith, Manager, Computers in Education Centre, Ontario Ministry of Education; Susan Tilley, CEMCORP; Peter Duynstee, CEMCORP; Mike Thomas, Burroughs Canada; Amanda Sun, Burroughs Canada; Lawrence Connelly, Brother Rice High School, St. John's, Newfoundland; Bruce Peters, Computer Consultant at the Toronto Board of Education; Gord Mahaffy and students at Northern Secondary School, Toronto, who participated in the photo session for the cover; and D. Michael Herriott and Robert Sutherby, founding members of the St. John's, Newfoundland, ICON Users' Group.

To all these and to the trainees, my colleagues in exploration in the test-sites, go my thanks and appreciation for support, advice, encouragement, assistance, forbearance, and conversation.

Very special thanks go to: Glenn Myers, President of CEMCORP; Ken Howarth, Vice-President of CEMCORP; Trudy L. Rising, Publisher, Science & Technology, John Wiley & Sons Canada Limited; and one whom I did not meet but who labored long over my scribblings: Val Daigen, Editorial Consultant, Toronto.

Reading someone else's manuscript, tolerating the typos, assessing the accuracy, suppressing the solecisms, and indicating improvements, can be a great chore. Therefore, to E. Bruce Peters, Acting Coordinator, Computer Studies and Applications, Toronto Board of Education, and to Frank H. Sweet of Kanacomp Computer Services, for his painstaking study of the material, go my warmest thanks.

John D. Herriott
St. John's, Newfoundland
April, 1985

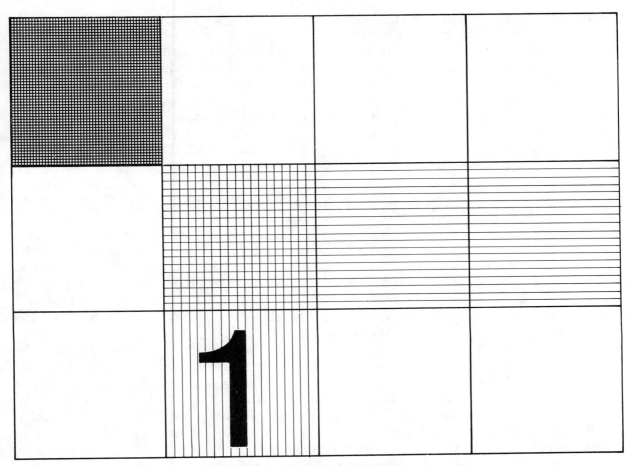

WHAT IS AN ICON?

I, the author, living perhaps a vast distance from you, cannot know whether you are familiar with computers, with just one computer, or with none at all. Likewise I cannot know whether you are sitting in front of an ICON or reading this before you encounter one. I am going to discuss the ICON as if you were indeed sitting before this new Canadian-made machine. If you are near one, sit in front of it with this book, and we will explore. If you are not, then read through this chapter seeing the machine in your mind's eye (with the aid of the photographs) and imagining that you are operating the equipment. As soon as you can, get to a machine and follow through with me.

I am going to assume that you are a first-time user. If you are not, then you can work through much of the material fairly rapidly, taking care nevertheless to correlate familiar practices with those required by the ICON and noting important differences from the machine or machines with which you have already worked. I will also assume that the system is already set up and ready to go. The LEXICON, the main unit of the system, should be switched on.

Follow the first part of this tour with your eyes only. You will soon get your digits busy! Give yourself an hour. Make sure that you are not going to be disturbed. You can cover quite a bit in this session.

THE ICON SYSTEM

The ICON is a complete computer and has all the necessary bits and pieces. However, it does not work alone (unless, of course, you are working with one of the stand-alone units; for the purposes of this book, I am assuming that you are using a full networking system consisting of a LEXICON and a number of ICONS).

The ICON is linked to a large, flat box known as a *fileserver*. Its name is LEXICON, a Greek word meaning "dictionary". It is also a full-fledged computer, yet it cannot work without its counterpart, the part you are sitting in front of. I will describe the LEXICON more fully in the next section.

The ICON and the LEXICON are linked by a length of coaxial cable. On the back of the fileserver, you will find two round sockets. The coaxial cable fits into these and runs to the ICONs. You may run one length of cable to an ICON in one part of the room and another, plugged into the second socket, to an ICON in another part of the room.

At the back of the ICON unit, on the pedestal, you will find a recessed array of sockets. Among them are two terminal sockets. The cable from the LEXICON plugs into one of them. You can now attach a second ICON to the first, in daisy-chain fashion, by plugging in a length of cable to the second socket. You can link a large number of ICONs in this way, in both directions from the LEXICON. The last ICON in each chain will have an extra socket. Into the spare socket must be plugged a small device called a *terminator*. THERE MUST BE A TERMINATOR IN ANY OTHERWISE UNUSED SOCKET, WHETHER ON ICON OR ON LEXICON. A CORRECTLY LINKED SYSTEM WILL HAVE *TWO* TERMINATORS.

On each ICON, again in the recessed socket panel, there are two AC outlets. One is marked "Switched". The AC three-pin plug attached to the monitor power cord is plugged into this. The second outlet, under the switched outlet, is there for you to plug the next ICON into the system, daisy-chaining the electrical power between parts of the system in the same fashion as the communications. Or you could plug a printer in the second outlet if you wished. You will find a similar outlet on the back of the LEXICON, and it is probably better to reserve that outlet, rather than the one on the ICON, for the printer; in a moment I will explain why.

Once more to the back of the ICON, where you will find a small multi-pin socket. Into this goes the plug from the monitor. The multi-pin socket and plug carry the signals from the computer to the monitor.

If you have a printer, it should be attached to the LEXICON. There are three blue sockets on the back of the LEXICON, and the leftmost (looking at the back of the unit) is the parallel socket. If you have a *parallel printer*, you must plug it into the parallel socket. The plug can be inserted only one way round. If you look at the plug from the printer and the socket on the LEXICON, you will see that each has a distinctive shape that matches the other. Each pin on the plug must enter a specific hole in the socket. The special shape of the plug-socket combination makes sure that there is no mix-up. It is impossible to insert the plug upside down, so do not try to force anything.

If you have a *serial printer*, the cable should be plugged into one of the serial sockets. The instructions that come with the printer will explain the difference and tell you how to plug the cable into the printer. Usually the parallel socket is on the outside of the printer case; the serial socket, inside the printer case. Consult the manual for the printer.

You can plug the printer directly into the ICON, but only if you have the correct sockets fitted. With the printer attached to the LEXICON, printing functions are available to all users. If the printer is attached to an ICON unit, however, printing functions will be available only to that particular ICON and to no others in the system, unless the commands you issue indicate otherwise. In addition, some of the facilities for printing directly from BASIC programs must be coded in special ways.

So there you are! Your system might look like the diagram in Figure 1.1.

THE LEXICON

The LEXICON (see Figure 1.2) should be placed on a firm table, away from places where it could be knocked or shaken. It should be in a dust-free environment that does not get too hot or too cold. What is comfortable for you will also be comfortable for your LEXICON.

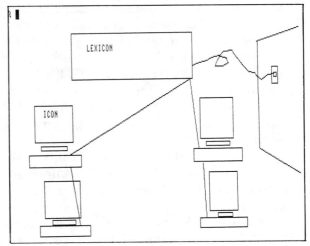

Figure 1.1 The ICON system.

Courtesy CEMCORP/Michael Lant

Figure 1.2 The LEXICON contains a hard disk and a floppy disk drive.

The LEXICON fileserver does most of the work in the ICON system. It contains, among other things, a device called a *hard disk*, which is nothing more than a massive storage device, constantly whirring round and

3

round (which is why the unit hums gently). The hard disk is rather like a tape-recorder that is always in a ready state — ready to record or play at the instant required.

In addition to the hard disk, the LEXICON has a diskette drive. Another name for the diskette drive is *floppy disk drive*. While the hard disk has a capacity of 10 megabytes (10 million characters: letters, numerals, punctuation marks, and spaces), the floppy disk drive has a capacity of only 640 kilobytes (640 thousand characters) — but that is plenty. These figures are based on a double-sided, double-density floppy disk that accommodates 96 tracks per inch (96 tpi). (Tracks are rather like the grooves on a phonograph record.) Some floppy disks allow for only 48 tpi. They work very well but provide only 320 kilobytes' storage.

The floppy disk drive is used for *backing up* (copying) important material — for example, student records or work — either to the floppy disk from the hard disk for independent storage, or to the hard disk from a floppy that may have been prepared on a system hundreds or thousands of miles away!

Access to the floppy will be needed relatively rarely by most users, and so the LEXICON can be placed in a fairly remote and secure place. For those who are likely to want constant access to the floppy disk drive, the ICON should be fairly close to the LEXICON. If the system you are using includes a stand-alone ICON, that is, an ICON with a floppy disk drive built into the front, then all backing up can be carried out from this station.

The LEXICON and the ICON are symbiotic units. They work together. The LEXICON, containing the hard disk and various other bits and pieces of electronic wizardry, drives the whole system. When you call up the various languages and talk to the operating system, when you deal with the text and graphics editors, the LEXICON manages it all for you.

The operating system just mentioned is, in this case, the QNX operating system. It looks after all the activities that the linked units can indulge in. You give the operating system an instruction, and it carries it out, just like that — unless, of course, you try to tell it something it does not understand. The computer is, after all, a relatively dumb creature, with only its operating system to guide it.

THE KEYBOARD

It is time to take a quick look at the keyboard (see Figure 1.3). In this chapter, I will describe only some features of the keyboard. I will describe the rest of the features in Chapter 2.

The keyboard has three main parts, and an important extra part tucked up in one corner.

Courtesy CEMCORP/Michael Lant

Figure 1.3   The ICON keyboard.

The Function Keys

Along the top, you will find a row of function keys. Ten of them are labeled from 1 to 10, with the prefix F. At each end, there is a key marked ACTION. You will be using those quite a lot when you come to use the text and graphics editors. There are two blank keys — keys with no labels. You will use them eventually.

The QWERTY Keyboard

Directly below the function keys, you will find the familiar QWERTY keyboard, so called because of the layout of the first five letter keys. The QWERTY keyboard is fairly standard for typewriters and now computers, but the ICON has some additions that should be noted.

To the left of the Q is a key with two arrows. This is the TAB key. The arrow, or *cursor*, on the screen will move five spaces to the right each time the TAB key is pressed. Under it, you will find the CTRL, or control, key. This key is used in conjunction with various other keys to perform special activities. Its use is often denoted by means of the ∧ symbol; thus, ∧**C** means press down the CTRL key and the letter C at the same time.

At the bottom left, there is a PAUSE key. This is used to hold material on the screen while you examine it; otherwise, it will scroll merrily up the screen, and you will not have time to read it.

Next to the PAUSE key there is a CAP LOCK key. It will light up when it is active, after it has been pressed.

To the right of the QWERTY keyboard, you will find RUBOUT and HELP keys, as well as a number of others that will be explained at appropriate times. Two letter keys produce French characters; the ICON is bilingual. Below these keys is the ENTER key.

Each time you are required to press either the ENTER or one of the ACTION keys, the words will be placed in special parentheses, like this:

⟨ENTER⟩
⟨ACTION⟩

In other words, you do not type the whole word, but merely press that key.

The Key-pad

The last section of the keyboard is the block on the extreme right, called a *numeric key-pad*, *hex-pad*, or just *key-pad*. This feature is common on computers for rapid input of figures. On the ICON, it is also used to control the cursor when editing BASIC, Pascal, and other programs and can be used for other purposes, too.

Now for the important extra part I spoke of!

The Trackball

Over on the right — you cannot have failed to notice it — is the *trackball*. Roll it under your fingers to get the feel of it. You will be using the trackball a great deal, in conjunction with the ACTION keys.

SWITCHING ON

Just above the keyboard, on a pedestal, is a screen. On the pedestal, just beside the word

ICON (in blue), you will find an amber toggle switch. Press the switch so that it lights up. (Some models may not have the word ICON on the pedestal, but the amber switch is obvious.)

On the lower right corner of the monitor housing, above the amber toggle switch you have just used, is a small rectangular push switch. Just above it there is a small round red light. If it is not on, push the switch so that it does come on.

The first image to appear will be a weird pattern. It will not make any sense to you, but it makes a lot of sense to the computer. Soon, numbers will appear, and then the screen will clear to show the logo ICON, as in Figure 1.4. The ICON is at your command!

Figure 1.4 The display you will see on the screen when the ICON is ready to be used.

SUMMARY

The two fundamental parts of the ICON system are the LEXICON, or fileserver, and the ICON, or terminal. A number of ICONs can be attached to a single LEXICON by means of coaxial cable. A printer can be attached to the ICON but is usually attached to the LEXICON instead.

The LEXICON drives the whole ICON system. It contains two storage devices: the hard disk and the floppy disk. The floppy disk drive backs up, or copies, material from one type of disk onto the other.

The keyboard of the ICON has three parts: the function keys (across the top), the QWERTY keyboard, and the numeric key-pad.

The QWERTY keyboard contains, in addition to the keys found on an ordinary typewriter, some special keys, including the ACTION and ENTER keys. When you see the word ACTION or ENTER in parentheses — ⟨ACTION⟩, ⟨ENTER⟩ — that means you should push the appropriate button, not type the word.

The numeric key-pad allows for rapid input of numbers and, under certain conditions, control of the cursor.

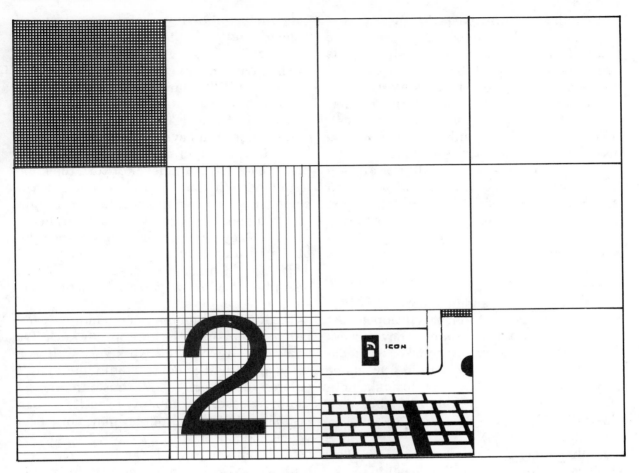

GETTING STARTED

ACCESSING DEMONSTRATION PROGRAMS

The ICON is switched on and is showing its logo. The word Login: is sitting there waiting for you to enter a special word that will allow you access to the system.

This business of a login name is important. It derives from the days when organizations did not own their own computers but rented time on a large installation. Company A would arrange to rent space on Computer XYZ. The firm would, in effect, open an account with the company that owned Computer XYZ. Company A would then be charged for the actual amount of connect time on the computer (in addition to any other charges that might be considered appropriate).

A similar situation exists on the ICON, except that users in schools are unlikely to be charged! You see, everyone is sharing the same space (a concept that will be expanded on in Chapter 4), and there must be some way of making sure that each individual has access to a portion of that space without getting things mixed up with whatever anyone else has stored there.

You will be given, if you do not already have, a personal login name and password (these will be discussed in detail in the next chapter). For the moment, however, you will take a tour of the ICON with a special login name for first-time users.

Type the word

icon

in lower-case letters, and then press **⟨ENTER⟩**. Immediately a percent sign % will appear just below the word **Login**: You now have access to the system. The percent sign % is called a *shell prompt*. Do not worry right now about why it is called a shell prompt. Just take note of the name. Now type the following very carefully:

cd /demo⟨ENTER⟩

Note the single space before the slash. The slash can be found under the question mark.

Again the shell prompt % will appear. The percent sign with no message indicates success in entering your command.

You have called up the demo directory. A *directory* is like a filing cabinet: it is a place where you store particular types of files. A *file* is any body of material, produced by you or by someone else, that is stored in the computer. A file can be an essay, a program in any one of the languages, or just a list of items.

What you will do next is access the sayer program, which is a file in the demo direc-tory. Do the following; that is, type the word "sayer" and press the **⟨ENTER⟩** key:

sayer⟨ENTER⟩

The sayer program was written by Dr. R.S. McLean of the Ontario Institute for Studies in Education. It allows you to hear the speech capabilities of the ICON.

Just under the keyboard and to the right, you will find either a small black knob or a black lever. Slide the lever or turn the knob to the right. (If you are in a crowded room or somewhere where noise would disturb others, you should probably use a set of headphones. They plug into the socket to the right of the volume control you have just used. The output is monophonic, so a set of stereo headphones will give you sound in only one ear!)

The ICON will announce both numbers and letters as you press the appropriate keys. Try a few. The ICON could work very well as a caller at a Bingo game! In a radio interview, I entered the letters "cbc", thus announcing the broadcasting company. (The ICON can also sing, but that program may not be on your system at first.)

Spell out some words, and then try combining words, or combining certain letters; try these, for example:

---

i c u⟨ENTER⟩
u c y⟨ENTER⟩
thir teen⟨ENTER⟩

Note the spaces between elements. You can build up quite a lot of phrases, even though every word or portion of a word will seem to be punched out at you.

When you have tired of hearing this (or been told to terminate the activity!) press the CTRL key (on the left of the QWERTY keyboard, the letters written in yellow) and the letter c. These actions will allow you to exit from the sayer program.

Now type and enter the following command:

line.bw

Make sure that all letters are in lower case, that the period is there between **line** and **bw**, and that there are no spaces. When you have finished watching the graphics display, press **(CTRL)** c once more to exit the program. You will find a variation on the display if you now type the following:

line.pack

Again, **(CTRL)** c will allow you to exit. Pressing any key you wish will freeze the display, and pressing **(ENTER)** will allow the motion to continue.

The following are items you might also like to try:

---

hanoi
line.color

Just type the name and press **(ENTER)**. If you are not working at a color machine, the line.color program will show an inverse video screen. In other words, the screen will turn amber, and the line patterns will appear as before. To revert to normal, you must again press **(CTRL)** c (∧c is the way that command is normally written) and then log out by typing **(CTRL)** d (∧d) **(ENTER)**, switching off the machine, and switching back on again after a few seconds. You will have to work through the login procedure once more, but the practice will be useful. The manner of getting out of color mode will probably have changed by the time this book is published, but that is the way with computers.

If you wish to see what files there are in the demo directory, type the command **ls**, which stands for "list sorted". To access one of the files, type its names and press **(ENTER)**.

MORE ABOUT THE KEYBOARD

As explained in Chapter 1, the ICON keyboard is set out rather like that of a typewriter. Some of you may have a little difficulty in finding certain items at first; you may be accustomed to looking in different places for some characters. For example, on some computers, the quotation marks are to be found above the number 2 on the top row of QWERTY keys. On the ICON, the quotes are in the more usual spot over on the right.

In Chapter 1, you learned that some characters on the keyboard perform special functions when combined with certain commands. Right now you will not use these keys. You will just hunt for them so that you will know where they are.

Along the bottom row, to the right of the space bar, you will find a key marked RUBOUT. This does exactly what the word indicates. Type something on the keyboard and then press **(RUBOUT)** once only. The last character will disappear. Now type a long string of letters — anything will do — and then press **(RUBOUT)**, keeping it pressed until you reach the beginning of your random letters.

To the right of the RUBOUT key, you will see a backward slash \ and a curious symbol ¦. These symbols are used under special circumstances, the ¦ probably being of greater use to you in the early stages than the \.

To the left of the question mark are the two symbols ⟨ and ⟩. They are the "less than"

9

and "greater than" symbols. Do not confuse them with brackets or braces, which are to be found at the right, on the same line as the QWERTY keys.

Directly below the bracket keys, you will find a Greek beta symbol, which doubles as the German double s sign, and, on Series II machines, an unmarked key with a small round spot on it. Press this key to see the spot light up in red. On Series III machines, this key is clearly marked CUR LOCK. This key activates the cursor control keys found on the key-pad—the keys with the arrows on them. They will be inoperative at present, having no effect on the screen. You will discover their use later.

The numbers on the key-pad are laid out in standard calculator form so that the keys lie under the fingers. The key-pad has its own ENTER key too, so that hand movement need not be too large.

At the bottom of the key-pad, there are INS and DEL keys. These keys are operative when the cursor lock is on.

Do note that zero and the letter o are not interchangeable on a computer. Zero has a slash through it, thus: Ø. There will be times when you will need to be absolutely sure of which is which so that there are no errors.

Above the bracket keys, you will see a left-arrow key. This will be used in the text editor. Do not confuse it with the RUBOUT key.

The function keys at the top serve specific purposes in some activities and can be programmed during others. There are two unmarked function keys that are always programmable. The text will indicate what can happen and when.

There is a key marked ESC on the left of the main QWERTY keyboard. This is the "escape" key and is used to exit from certain activities.

Explore the keys, using them as you wish. Do not worry if nothing seems to happen, and do not be concerned if something untoward happens. Just take things slowly and observe the results.

Do not assume anything. Do not expect keys to perform the same function that you may be used to. The way computer keyboards perform differs according to the notions of the designers. The ICON keyboard is fairly standard for large machines; smaller computers have strange idiosyncracies that can create confusion for those who are not used to working with a variety of machines.

▓ SUMMARY ▓

Every user needs a unique word — a login name — in order to have access to and reserve space in the ICON system.

The ICON responds to commands that are typed in lower-case letters. Some commands include a period or underscore mark (although none with underscores were introduced in this chapter). There may be no spaces in a command. Commands are issued after the appearance of the shell prompt %.

The ICON is supplied with a number of demonstration programs that display the various features of the equipment, and these programs are available even to users without their own login names. Simply log in with the name **icon**. Then change to the demo directory by typing the name of the file and then pressing **(ENTER)**. Some of the files that may be in the directory in your system were listed in the chapter.

More special features of the ICON keyboard were introduced.

Courtesy CEMCORP/Michael Lant

11

THE SITE ADMINISTRATOR

In any large-scale operation, there must always be someone who is in ultimate control. With many users capable of being accommodated on the ICON system, there must be a means of checking that the system is in full operation, that the files do not get in a mess, that files are cleaned up if they do get in a mess, and that generally things are running smoothly.

In this chapter, I will describe the activities for which that individual, called the *site administrator* or *system manager*, is usually responsible. Some of the activities are allowed for general users, and soon there will be a third type of user. It is likely, if you are a student or employee, that you will be allowed access to certain activities. Whether or not the functions apply to you, it is important for you to understand them. If you have your own system, you will automatically be a site administrator and should read this chapter thoroughly and practice the examples. In my opinion, there is no reason why a student should not be allowed to perform some of the site administrator activities.

EDITING THE PASSWORD FILE

Each person using the ICON system must log in using a specific *login name*. In addition, for extra protection, a *password* may be used. A login name/password combination is just like a double lock on a door. First you type your login name after the prompt Login:. If the ICON system recognizes your login name, you will then be asked for your password. Typing your password (and pressing **(ENTER)**) will allow you to use the computer.

The ICON system can accommodate any number of login/password combinations in addition to that of the site administrator. Some of the names, such as the name ''icon'' you used in Chapter 2, can be used by large numbers of people. Just think for a moment how many people will be reading this text and using the login name ''icon''. Almost everyone who uses the ICON system will have begun by using that login name.

One of the functions of the site administrator is to provide other users with login names and passwords. This is done in secret so that no one other than the user and the site administrator knows that user's password.

The site administrator or manager has a special login name and password. These are supplied with the equipment when it arrives, but they can be changed — and the password

in particular *should* be changed — regularly by the site administrator once he or she is fully familiar with the editing of the password file. There is really no need to change the login name, but there are good security reasons for changing the password. Although computer experts stand a very good chance of finding out what a password is, some passwords are more difficult than others to discover. Choosing login names and passwords should, therefore, be done very carefully. I have worked with a group of people who used their last names as the login names and their first names as the passwords. Nothing could be easier than to get at their files!

It is preferable to choose an unusual word for your password — not too long or too hard to spell, yet not readily guessable. You could try the trick of leaving out vowels in the password. Just be sure your password is not too complicated for *you* to remember!

Those of you who are site administrators will know the login name and password that came with the system. I shall not use any of those that I know, so that your security may be preserved. When I tell you to log in as site administrator, you will know what to do.

To protect your secrecy as site administrator, the password will not appear on the screen. The site administrator shell prompt, which is a dollar sign ($), not a percent sign, will appear on the screen.

One of the functions of the site manager is to edit the password file, assigning login names and passwords. Make sure that no one is able to look over your shoulder for the next part. Secrecy is essential.

First, log in as site administrator. Then change to the configuration directory by typing the following:

cd /config⟨ENTER⟩

Again, note the space between **cd** and the slash.

The next thing to type is this:

ed pass⟨ENTER⟩

On the screen, you will see a list of users and their passwords. (Now you understand the need for secrecy!)

You need to add names to the end of the file, so type the letter **z**. This will automatically bring you to the end of the password file.

Now type the letter **i**. This puts you in the insert mode.

Now type the login name chosen by a new user. Use the RUBOUT key if you make an error. Press **⟨ENTER⟩** when you have typed the name correctly.

Now press the double-arrow, or TAB, key once. (This is the key with two arrows on it next to the letter Q.) Then type the password chosen by the new user and press **⟨ENTER⟩**.

Press the **⟨TAB⟩** key once more, and then assign a number, taking as your cue the number of the last entry; thus, if the last entry is 10, choose 11. Make a note of the number.

Press **⟨ENTER⟩**. Then press the **⟨TAB⟩** key once more. Then type the following:

/user/(loginname)⟨ENTER⟩

The words you see in parentheses in the commands throughout this book are words that will vary from user to user. We call such words *variables*. Do not type the parentheses or the words inside them. Just type your choice of variable. In this case, the login name will be the first name you typed. Thus, if the login name is Fitzwilliam, that is the name you type after the second slash:

/user/fitzwilliam⟨ENTER⟩

Press **⟨TAB⟩** once more and then **⟨ENTER⟩**, thus leaving a blank line. Then press the ESC key.

The next thing to do is press the letter **q**, just by itself. Note that there was no need to press **⟨ENTER⟩** for the last two items. You should now have an asterisk * on the screen. Type the letter **w**. This "writes", or stores, what you have just typed.

Again you should press **⟨ENTER⟩**, and you will see the asterisk once more.

This time type a letter **q** followed by **⟨ENTER⟩**. You should now have the site administrator shell prompt $ on the screen.

Now you must make a directory for the new user by typing the following:

mkdir /user/(loginname)⟨ENTER⟩

After a short wait, the site administrator shell prompt $ will return to you, and you must then assign the owner number by typing the following command:

chattr/user/(loginname)   o = (number)
⟨ENTER⟩

Note that it is the letter **o**, *not* the zero, and that the number will be that assigned on line three of the password file you just edited.

Check over the line to make sure it is correct. Then log out by pressing ∧**d**. The word Login: should now appear, and your new user can now access the ICON via his or her own account name.

The process of editing the password file must be approached with caution. If you use the method just described, follow the directions carefully each time. If there is a whole raft of new names to be entered, you will become adept at it. But, if you do not have to edit the file for some weeks, it is a good idea to have the instructions right beside you just to make sure.

The fifth line need not be left blank. It can be used to indicate a language the user wants to work with. (To use any of the languages available on the ICON system, you must "load" it onto your ICON by giving a command. You will learn how to do that in Chapter 4.)

There is a simpler means of entering new login names and passwords. Again, you must be logged on as site administrator and change to the configuration directory. This time, however, merely type this command:

new_user⟨ENTER⟩

There may be no spaces, and be sure to type an underscore, not a hyphen.

You will be prompted through the steps by means of screen directions. The first one will be this:

Enter new login name: (type ⟨CNTRL/C⟩ to abort)

Although the screen shows a capital C, you should type a lower-case **c**!

At this point, you must enter the new login name — for example, **piano**.

The ICON will then ask if the new user should be a site administrator, the answer to which would normally be no, indicated by typing the letter **n**.

There is no need to assign a user number, for this is provided by the ICON new_user program.

You will now be instructed to type the new password. Again, here is an example: **fund**.

You will be asked to retype the password just to be sure.

The last question will be whether you want the login directory to be different from "/user/piano", the answer to which will normally be no.

The process will then begin again, with this question:

Add another new user? (y/n):

Obviously, the answer is **y** if you do and **n** if you do not wish to add another new login name and password. If you answer no, then the site administrator shell prompt will appear on the screen. Log out and then log in again using the new names you have just entered, in order to make sure that each login name and password works properly. It will, of course, but it is important that you be assured of that.

Just as important as adding new users is the ability to delete those who, for one reason or another, no longer have access to the ICON system. The easiest way is to use the **delete_user** facility.

In order to practice this, first create a new-user account using the login name **gold** and the password **mine** by means of the new_user facility you have just encountered. You must be logged on as site administrator, so do that first if you are not already in that directory.

The ICON will prompt you through the steps.

When you have finished, check that the new name and password work (they will, but you may need assurance!) by logging out and then logging in again under the new names. Alternatively, you may issue this command:

p pass

This will cause the entire password file to appear on the screen, but only if you are logged on as site administrator. You will find the new name at the end of the file.

Now issue this command:

delete_user

The screen will ask you to type in the login name you wish to delete. Type **gold**.

Immediately the ICON will tell you that you must delete the directory called "gold" before you can delete the name from the password file. If you recall, when you created this new name, you were asked if you wanted the directory name to be different from "gold". You typed an **n**, but only because I told you to. The point about directories and their names will become clearer in the next chapter and need not hold you up at present. In order to delete this directory, you must type this command:

drel /user/gold⟨ENTER⟩

The dollar sign, the site administrator prompt, will reappear on the screen, and you can go ahead and type this command:

delete_user

Note the underscore, as in the **new_user** command.

The deed is done. Examine the password file once more to check that the new name is now no longer there.

Practice this if you are a site administrator. If you are not a site administrator, try to practice it just to see the messages you receive! The statement **permission denied** seems rather chilling, doesn't it? It just would not do for any user to be able to delete other users. This is one of the reasons why the site administrator function exists. As I mentioned before, there can be more than one person having access as site administrator. (You will remember that the new_user utility asks whether the new user should be a site administrator.) The ICON arrives with a site administrator login name and password, but new ones can be added for security purposes. It should be clear that anyone who knows the site administrator login name and password combination can have access to the whole system, whether entitled to or not.

The password file is just like any other file on the ICON. It is just a special place where a list of the users is kept. However, it also controls use of the system by checking to see whether the person trying to access other files is allowed to or not. Each time a user logs on, the operating system calls up the password file and passes through it to see if that name exists. Type in a name that you can be sure is not on the file — **polycarpus**, for example — just to see what happens.

SETTING UP GENERAL-USER ACCOUNTS

General-user accounts allow a great number of users to use the same login name. The "icon" login name is one example. The site administrator can establish other general-user accounts.

A computer is a device for communication. It can store all sorts of information, placed there by one set of individuals and retrieved by another set; or a group of people can exchange information among themselves. An ICON set up in the school library or resource center could be used for, among other things, access to a variety of bits and pieces of information. Inasmuch as the information is open for general use, a general-user account, with or without password, could be established for those wishing to access the information.

Let us say that the information or data store contains a section on science. The login name could be the word "science". When the user types this word, he or she is led directly to that directory and has no need to pass through a whole series of directories to get there, with the chance of mistyping commands or even forgetting what the commands are.

A computer is a vastly versatile teaching device. There is a lot of material that falls into the category of *computer-assisted instruction* (*CAI*). This type of software leads the student, young or old, through the material in carefully graded steps.

CAI material can be set up in general-user accounts. Let us say that you have a set of materials for Grade X math. The login name could be "gradex", the password could be "math", and the fifth line could directly load BASIC, or whatever language the CAI material happens to be written in.

If you imagine the use such material would be put to over the years, you can see that very many more than a mere 254 users would have to be accommodated. (The number 255 is the largest number that can be represented by an eight-bit *binary number*. Number 255 is reserved for the site administrator, and so there are just 254 numbers left.)

Who, then, would have user accounts? Some of the teaching staff would, of course. The site administrator would have another account — for site-management purposes, *not* for his or her personal use. In addition, one group of senior students would have their own accounts for programming, and another would have accounts for advanced word processing; these accounts could be assigned according to perceived need.

CHANGING ATTRIBUTES OF A FILE

Unless other arrangements are made, any file can be read by any user, whether the file belongs to him or her or not. It is one of the functions of the site administrator to make the alternative arrangements. Indeed, any user can protect files so that they cannot be read by others. There will be situations where files must be kept secure.

The special arrangements come under the category of "changing attributes of a file". An *attribute* is a letter such as w, which stands for "write", or r, which stands for "read". If a file has the w attribute, the user may write to the file — that is, store further information in it. If the file has r, then the user may read the file. If these attributes are missing, then the user may neither read the file nor store more information in it.

One need not be in the site administrator account to change attributes of one's own files. I explain the procedure here only because it is something that the site administrator might wish to advise on in the early stages of ICON system use, and supervise as a general practice.

In order to change the attributes of a file, you must be in your home directory. Type these letters:

cd⟨ENTER⟩
Now type this command:
files + v⟨ENTER⟩

Note the space after the word **files**.

There may be only a few files generated in your home directory, but they are still worth looking at. If you have no files in your account at present, then change to the directory containing ICON *utilities*. (A utility is a program that performs an activity that makes life easier for the user.) To change to this directory, type the following command:

cd /util

The command you issued asked for full details — verbose, in fact (that is what the **v** stands for) — on the files in that directory.

If there are a lot of files, then you will have to use the PAUSE key to examine a particular file. Figure 3.1 shows the sort of thing you will see.

```
% files +v
  Blk  X Loc  Grp Own Attr  G-Perm-O     Date      Time    Name
   35  1 1fce 000 006 m-awr ----- ----r  28-Jun-84  2:01am  animation2.t
    4  1 1ff1 000 006 m-awr ----- ----r  28-Jun-84  2:19am  animation3.t
   62  2 2fcb 000 006 m-awr ----- ----r  22-Sep-84  3:45am  casablanca.t
   44  2 2852 000 006 m-awr ----- ----r   4-Aug-84  5:25am  desert.t
   18  1 2f2f 000 006 m-awr ----- ----r  22-Sep-84  2:28am  dingdong.t
   10  1 2cda 000 006 m-awr ----- ----r  28-Aug-84  6:34am  dog.t
    9  1 253a 000 006 m-awr ----- ----r   3-Aug-84  5:35am  door.bas
    2  1 2544 000 006 m-awr ----r ----r  12-Mar-85  8:16am  examp.t
   63  1 2037 000 006 meawr ----- -e--r  23-Jun-84 11:33pm  figure
   44  3 1d5a 000 006 m-awr ----- ----r  23-Jun-84 11:13pm  figure.bas
    9  1 1d46 000 006 m-awr ----- ----r  23-Jun-84 11:13pm  figure.t
   56  2 2dd7 000 006 m-awr ----- ----r   4-Sep-84  5:38pm  girl.t
   23  1 2012 000 006 m-awr ----- ----r  28-Jun-84  7:26pm  goodanim.t
   44  1 24f0 000 006 m-awr ----- ----r   2-Aug-84  8:18am  hill.t
   34  2 297d 000 006 m-awr ----- ----r   4-Aug-84  5:52am  illust.t
   20  1 2578 000 006 meawr -e--r -e--r   9-Mar-85  6:39am  karen
   20  1 2146 000 006 m-awr ----r ----r   9-Mar-85  6:38am  karen.c
    2  1 233b 000 006 m-awr ----r ----r   9-Mar-85  6:46am  karen1
   45  1 2e49 000 006 m-awr ----- ----r  10-Sep-84  4:29pm  lady.t
   38  2 1ddb 000 006 m-awr ----- ----r  23-Jun-84  6:20pm  man.t
   25  1 251c 000 006 meawr -e--r -e--r   2-Mar-85  4:41am  map
```

Figure 3.1   Sample list of files produced by the **files +v** command.

Reading across the top, you see the number of blocks taken up on the disk, an **X** (the number of links between this and other files), the location on the disk, and then the group owner number of the file. Next to the group owner number, in this case **000**, is the user's owner number, here **007**. The site administrator's owner number will always be **255**. (The site administrator will have a different number for personal files.) Normally, the number in the owner column will be the same as the one assigned in the password file.

Next you see a column marked Attr. These are the attributes of the files with respect to the owner of the files—that is, what the owner may do to the files. Each letter stands for a particular attribute: m = modify, a = append, w = write, r = read.

In the next column is what other users are permitted to do. Normally, other users will be allowed only to read the file, not to execute it (e), write to it, append it, modify it, or otherwise tamper with it, unless the owner gives specific permission to do so.

The next column shows the date of creation of the file, the following column the time of creation, and finally the name of the file.

In order to remove, let us say, the read permission from a file, you would use the command **chattr**, which is short for "change attributes" and is usually pronounced "chatter".

You do not have to be a site administrator to perform this operation on your own files; in fact, as noted above, you should be in your home directory with the shell prompt % on the screen waiting for your command. The all-powerful site administrator can change attributes on any files.

Part of the way down the list shown in Figure 3.1, you will notice a file called rich-ard. If I wished to remove the read permission from that file, I would type the following command:

    chattr richard po = -r⟨ENTER⟩

or

    chattr richard pg = -r⟨ENTER⟩

(The option **po** refers to permission for the owner; **pg** to permission for the group.)

Alternatively, if I wished to add write and append permissions to the file — if, say, it were a CAI program — I would issue the following command:

    chattr richard po (or **pg**) **= + w + a** ⟨ENTER⟩

BACKING UP FILES

One of the many tasks of a site administrator is to see that disk space is used efficiently. Actually, the ICON system does most of this automatically. What it cannot tell is whether the material stored on the disk is important or not, or whether it can be removed or stored elsewhere.

Storing files elsewhere is easy: you use the diskette. You will have noticed the floppy-disk-drive slot on the right-hand side of the LEXICON. The process is called *backup* and can be performed by users other than the site administrator, as long as the procedure is followed exactly. It is probably unwise for young beginning users to do this, for errors can prove quite frustrating. And only the site administrator may backup *all* the files. Individual users may backup only their own files.

Backing Up All the Files

As soon as possible after delivery of the ICON system, site administrators should backup all the system files according to the plan that follows. (This plan uses the ICON text editor, which I will discuss in Chapter 6. If you are not familiar with the use of the text editor, skip this section and come back to it when you are.)

Log in as site administrator.

Change directory to the /util directory.

Type this command:

    edit sysback⟨ENTER⟩

You are now in the text editor, complete with icons.

Place the cursor at the top left corner of the page, and then type *all* of the following:

```
clearscreen
type      This is a command file. Its function is to perform a
type       backup of the entire set of system files to a diskette.
type      You will be prompted when insertion of
type      diskettes is required. Obey all instructions carefully.
type      You will need 4 new diskettes, already formatted.
type          If you do not have formatted diskettes, then exit from
type      this utility now and return to it when the diskettes
type      are ready.
type          Insert the diskette for the /boot and /cmds files.
[1] dinit 2
backup /boot 2:/boot +a +d +o
backup /cmds 2:/cmds +a +d +o
type          Write the following on a diskette label and attach it
type      to the diskette:
type          /boot
type          /cmds
type          Insert the diskette for the /config, /icons,
type      /languages, /lib, /mathlib, /speech, /sys directories
type      and files.
[1] dinit 2
backup /config 2:/config +a +d +o
backup /icons 2:/icons +a +d +o
backup /languages 2:/languages +a +d +o
backup /lib 2:/lib +a +d +o
backup /mathlib 2:/mathlib +a +d +o
backup /speech 2:/speech +a +d +o
backup /sys 2:/sys +a +d +o
type      Remove the diskette and label it 'System disk II' and
type      list the contents.
type      Now insert the diskette for /util
[1] dinit 2
backup /util 2:/util +a +d +o
type      Remove the diskette and label it 'System disk III'
type      and list the contents.
type      Now insert the diskette for /demo
[1] dinit 2
backup /demo 2:/demo +a +d +o
```

```
type            Remove the diskette, label it 'System disk IV' and
type            list the contents.
type            Now insert the diskette for /sampler
[1] dinit 2
backup /sampler 2:/sampler +a +d +o
type            The system files backup procedure is now complete.
type            Make sure each diskette is clearly labeled.
type            Add the current date of backup.
type            Store the diskettes in a safe place.
```

Check over the above very carefully. Altering material is very simple with the ICON text editor. When you are certain that it is absolutely correct, save the program by placing the cursor over the door icon and pressing **(ACTION)**.

In order that the program may be executed, you must provide that attribute. The site administrator shell prompt will have been returned, so simply enter the following command:

chattr sysback a = + e⟨ENTER⟩

Now log out.

The foregoing is a clear example of how to use the QNX operating system to do a chore for you. There will be more details on QNX commands in other chapters, but it might interest you to note two new ones here: **type** and **clearscreen**. The latter can be issued directly from the keyboard. To try this, type something on the screen or issue an **ls** command to place something on the screen. Press **(ENTER)** to see the % prompt, and then issue the command:

clearscreen

The screen will clear, leaving the % sign behind.

The **type** command can be given directly after the %, but there is little point to doing so. Try it by typing the following command:

type This is the type command⟨ENTER⟩

The words This is the type command appear immediately.

It is much more useful to use the command in a QNX program (properly called a *command file*) such as the backup procedure I have described. Try this:

edit example⟨ENTER⟩

The editor having been invoked, type the following:

type This is an example of the ''type'' command

Save the text and leave the editor.

To allow the program to be executed, change the attribute as follows:

chattr example a = + e⟨ENTER⟩

Now issue this command:

example⟨ENTER⟩

The screen will clear, and the message This is an example of the ''type'' command will appear.

Formatting and Initializing Floppy Disks

A blank disk must be prepared magnetically by the computer in which it is to be used. The disk is divided up into magnetic sections that contain the data. This process is called *formatting and initialization.*

Formatting and initialization of floppy disks will probably remain in the domain of the site administrator in the early stages of operation but can be assigned to senior students or other staff at the discretion of the site administrator. These processes require knowledge of the site administrator login name and password. The procedure is quite simple but requires certain precautions.

The main precaution to take is to ensure that *no other station is in use during the formatting/initialization process.*

The site administrator shell prompt $ should be on the screen, after which you type this:

cd /util⟨ENTER⟩
Then type this:
[1] fdformat 2

The notation at the beginning of this last command consists of a left square bracket, the numeral 1, and a right square bracket. The numeral is called the node number. Do not worry about this—but do read the "Note" in the Preface.

The floppy disk should be double-sided, double-density, 96 tracks per inch (96 tpi). Do not be tempted to use single-sided disks with or without an extra notch and location hole punched in them! Disks are manufactured with both sides prepared with recording medium. They are then checked on both sides. Those disks with one poor side are sold as single-sided; those with both sides good are sold as double-sided.

The floppy disk is then inserted *with the small square notch down, and the label facing the left.* If you are right-handed, your thumb will be over the label.

Be very careful with floppy disks. They are as delicate to handle as long-playing records. Do not touch any exposed surface of the disk. Handle the black cover only.

When you have inserted the disk, close the lever by moving it to the right. Then follow the instruction you see on the screen, which is simply to press **⟨ENTER⟩**.

The small, round, red light on the floppy disk drive casing will come on and stay on for approximately sixty seconds, during which time messages will appear on the screen indicating that each track is being formatted. *Do nothing whatsoever while this light is on.* When formatting is complete, the site administrator shell prompt $ will reappear.

The next command will initialize the disk and must be entered very carefully. Be sure that what you have on the screen corresponds exactly with the command printed here before pressing **⟨ENTER⟩**:

[1] dinit 2⟨ENTER⟩

The numeral **2** refers to the floppy disk drive. If you omit it, the system will think you are referring to the hard disk. Do not omit the numeral **2**!

A message will be returned to you telling you how many blocks are available to you. Unless you wish to abort the operation, press **⟨ENTER⟩** again. When the red light goes off, you may check that the procedure has been carried out correctly by typing the following:

files 2:/⟨ENTER⟩

Note the space before the numeral **2**. The result of this command should be something like this:

Blk	Date	Time	Name
1	14-Oct-84	7:11am	2:/bitmap
Total blocks:1		Total files:1	

The next command is not essential but checks how much space is left on the floppy:

query 2:/⟨ENTER⟩

The response should be this:

1276 free blocks (0% full)

In order to make backups of the system files, three formatted disks are required, each containing specific portions. The backup copies should be kept in a metal box away from stray electrical influences of any kind. There is a temperature and humidity tolerance limit for floppies. The upper limit is 50°C, and there is also a lower limit. Do not store the floppies in a refrigerator.

Backing Up User Files

Backing up user files is relatively straightforward. A floppy disk should be ready, formatted and initialized.

Let us say that you are "jones" and that you have a file named "henry" that you wish to backup on the floppy. The command you issue will be as follows:

backup /user/jones 2:/jones p = henry +d +a ⟨ENTER⟩

The ICON will prompt you to insert the floppy into the drive. When you have done this, press **(ENTER)**, and the ICON will display a message indicating that the procedure is being carried out. The shell prompt % will be returned when the operation is complete.

The letters at the end of the command line mean specific things.

p = is the command to copy a specific file that is named. In the example given, the file is "henry". You could have specified any name there, of course, or you could have left the **p =** without a file name, in which case all files would have been copied.

+a commands that all dates of the specified files be copied.

+d commands that the dates of copied files be preserved on the copy. Should you have a number of versions of a particular file — say, a program you are developing — it is useful to be able to identify them by their dates. Remember the **files +v** command that showed you the attributes, permissions, and so on (Figure 3.1)? One of the columns showed you the date the file was created.

+o commands that the owner number be preserved in the backup. You will recall that the owner number is in the fourth column of the "files +v" listing.

The process of transferring files from the floppy disk to the hard disk is just as straightforward.

backup 2:/jones 1:/user/jones p = henry +a +d +o⟨ENTER⟩

In every case, commands follow this order: first the command, then the source (in the last example, the floppy, denoted by **2:/ jones**), then the destination (in this case, the hard disk, denoted by **1:/user/jones**), followed by the file name and all the rest.

Reasons for Backing Up Files

Among the systems files, you will find a selection of demonstration programs of various kinds. The actual nature of the programs will vary over a period of time, some being expunged and replaced by either new versions or altogether new programs. Some of the programs will be familiar to users of other machines. The programs are in the public domain and have been translated for use on the ICON.

I have found it best to keep those programs collected in a directory called "sampler", all on one disk (and the backup utility provided above does just that). The other systems files can be shared by two of the other three disks.

There may well be occasions when, for some reason or other, you lose the systems files — power failures are a notorious source of frustration — and the backup floppies will be your saving grace!

Frequent backup of user files is also advisable for the same reason. You do not want to lose valuable material when backups are so simple. You could try to produce a general backup utility, using the format shown in sysback, which prompts you for the various bits of information. You will need to use the command **copy** in certain spots to allow for input from the keyboard.

It is possible that, with a large number of users accessing the system, the hard disk will become full or nearly so. Unused files should be packed up on floppies and then deleted from the hard disk. The commands for deletion of files and directories can be found in Chapter 4 and in the list of QNX commands at the back of the book. Note that it is occasionally necessary to re-initialize the hard disk and reload the systems files from the diskettes — another good reason to keep the originals and the backups very safe!

If the system contains CAI programs that are to some degree time-dependent, they can be removed when not required. For example, there may be a series on Grade 11 math, some parts of which will be useful only during the first term. To keep them all on the hard disk when not required is clearly a waste of valuable space. Ten megabytes may seem to be unlimited space, but of course it is not.

SHARING THE RESPONSIBILITIES

The site administrator responsibilities must not be taken lightly, and a good deal of thought and consideration must be given to the question of whom to share the responsibilities with.

In some situations, there can be several people with access to the site administrator login name and password. Alternatively, several (but not too many!) different site administrator login names and passwords might exist, as indicated earlier in the chapter. People do fall sick, and it can be a nuisance if no one knows how to get at something in an emergency.

▓▓▓▓▓▓▓▓▓▓▓▓ **SUMMARY** ▓▓▓▓▓▓▓▓▓▓▓▓

The site administrator is responsible for a variety of special activities. Some, but not all, may be assigned to responsible users. It is best for the site administrator to become thoroughly familiar with activities such as backup before allowing general users to carry them out.

One of the functions of the site administrator is to add users' chosen login names and passwords to the password file, which is in the configuration directory. There are two ways of doing this — by editing the password file with the command **ed pass** or by issuing the command **new_user**. Both methods serve to create a directory for the new user.

Site administrators can establish general-user accounts in the same way as they establish individual-user accounts. The only difference is that the login name of a general-user account is known by many people, not just by one.

The attributes of a file are the activities its owner and others are permitted to perform on it. Any user can change the attributes of his or her own files by issuing the commands **files +v** and **chattr**. Only the site administrator can change the attributes of any file.

Another responsibility of the site administrator is to backup the files from the hard disk to the floppy disk, either to make room on the hard disk or to preserve copies in case of power failures. The first step is to prepare the floppy disk by formatting — with the command **[1] fdformat 2** — and initializing — with the command **[1] dinit 2**. Never issue either of these commands without the numeral **2**.

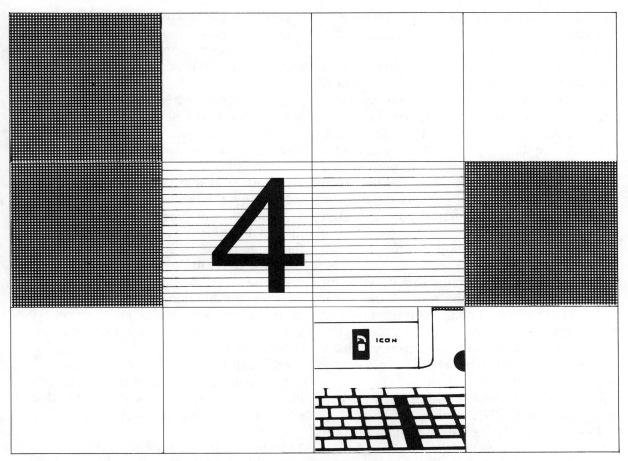

THE QNX OPERATING SYSTEM

HOW THE SYSTEM WORKS

The ICON is a complex system, just like a large organization, performing a great many functions very quickly and efficiently. The one function it cannot perform is yours: directing operations.

The ICON can also be likened to a vast, empty warehouse. At one end of the warehouse there is a group of offices with the appropriate personnel just waiting to help you fill up the empty space with whatever you wish.

The strange thing about the warehouse is that it can accommodate a large quantity of things belonging to a great variety of people, and yet each person is unable to see what other people have stored there, unless specific permission is granted for them to do so. The manager and staff, the operating system, see to this.

You are going to store something in this warehouse, but first you must claim an area for yourself. You give notice to the manager that you wish to be given a space. The manager orders one of the staff to do as you request. The staff member puts up a sign with your name on it. Next you say you want a portion of this space to be devoted to books. Another member of the staff marks out the portion you have chosen and puts up a sign that says ''Books''.

Consider this an analogy to the way the ICON works.

When you began using the ICON, you signed on by typing the word **icon** in response to the word Login:. You then moved to the directory called ''demo'' by typing the command **cd /demo**; and from there you have wandered through a series of files all neatly stacked under the demo directory. You found the file called ''sayer'', which allowed you to operate the ICON's mouth.

In effect, you first of all entered a portion of the warehouse called ''demo'' and then walked up and down the stacks of shelves looking at what was stored there, except that it was the shelves that moved, each one being quite independent of the others and able to move to your spot instantly!

CREATING DIRECTORIES AND FILES

If you have just been playing with the speech demonstration, you must move out of that directory — that is, that portion of the warehouse — and return to the original demo section.

Just type the following after the %:
cd ∧
The computer responds by showing another shell prompt, the % sign, like this:
%
Just to check where you are, type in the letters **wmi** (which stand for ''Where am I?''):
wmi
The computer responds with a message:
/user/demo
This tells you that you are in the directory called ''user/demo''.

Another shell prompt appears. Now you make a directory of your own (you can change the name later), by issuing this command:
mkdir herriott
At the next shell prompt (%), you issue another command to change directory, to the new one that you have called ''herriott''. (See if you can remember what the command is before looking at the next line!)
cd herriott
Now ask the computer to tell you which directory you are in. How do you do that? It is just three letters, remember?
wmi
The computer responds with this:
user/demo/herriott
Now you know that you are in the directory called ''herriott'', which is actually a subdirectory of the directory called ''user/demo''.

Now that you have reserved some space under your own name (well, under my name, actually, but you will change that shortly), you ought to put something there. Let us say you wish to put a pile of books there, or at least their titles.

Enter the following (after the shell prompt, which should be sitting there patiently):
ed books
The layout of the screen changes!

Enter the letter **i** (and press **⟨ENTER⟩**, of course!).

Now you can type in some text. You have called this part of your directory (which is actually a file) "books", and so you should put some books there. Type these titles:

The Bible
Shakespeare's Collected Works
Huckleberry Finn
The Memoirs of Sherlock Holmes
Anne of Green Gables

You can add to these if you wish, or you can stop right there and press **⟨ESC⟩** (recall where that is?) and **q** at the same time. Immediately you will see a new symbol on the screen:

*

Type the letter **w** and press **⟨ENTER⟩**.
Another * will appear.
Type a letter **q** (again), followed by **⟨ENTER⟩**.
The shell prompt will return.

You have just created a file called "books", which is stored under your directory called "herriott".

The command **ed** allows you to create, or "edit", the file, or list of book titles. There are other, more convenient, ways to do this that will be dealt with later on. The combination command **⟨ESC⟩** and the letter **q** allows you to "quit" entering data. The letter **w** stands for "write", because you must write the information to a file. Until you issue this command, the titles you have so carefully typed are in a computerworld limbo. The second letter **q** tells the computer that you do not wish to add anything more and wish to quit the editor completely.

Now make another file. Remember that you are still in the same part of your "warehouse", so that the new file will be under that management, or directory.

---

ed clothes⟨ENTER⟩
i⟨ENTER⟩

Now type the following:

---

suits
shirts
socks
boots
ties
⟨ESC⟩q
w
q

And once more you see the shell prompt %.

Now make a new directory in which you will keep your stamps. (Maybe you don't collect stamps, but copy what is printed here so that there is no confusion. You can change everything later.)

At the shell prompt, which is still sitting there patiently, type the following:

---

mkdir stamps
cd stamps
ed British
i
1840-1904 Victorian
1904-1910 Edwardian
⟨ESC⟩q
w
q
ed Canadian
i
Newfoundland
Nova Scotia

New Brunswick
(ESC)q
w
q

That will keep your stamps together under the directory "stamps", so that they will not be confused with books or clothes.

CREATING YOUR OWN FILES

As you know, each ICON user can be provided with his or her own login name and password. This is like having your own pass-key to the warehouse, or, to use a more up-to-date analogy, it is like the bank cards that allow you to get in through the bank doors after hours. On each bank card there is a number that the bank's computer recognizes as belonging to you and you alone. The number allows you access to your account. Before you can gain access to the computer unit, you must be provided with a card and a number. These are provided by an official at the bank.

Likewise with the ICON. The teacher in charge of the ICON system must provide you with a login name and password. You must ask to be provided with a special login name and password. For general purposes, you will not need one and can continue to create the sample files under the /user/icon directory. You will delete all the files eventually so that there will be no confusion.

If you have a login name and password, log out from the /user/icon directory by pressing **(CTRL)** and the letter **D** at the same time. The word Login: will appear on the screen once more. Type your login name and

press **(ENTER)**. The word password will then appear. Type in your password, being very careful, and then press **(ENTER)**. You will then see the shell prompt %.

If you do not have a personal login name and password, do not worry. There is a good reason for you not to have them at this time. Merely continue the next exercise without them, using the general "icon" login name. First, make a directory with your name, as follows:

mkdir (yourname)

Then change to that directory by typing this:

cd (yourname)

Now go through the whole sequence of directory and file creation using your own name and things you would like to store in files.

First, make a directory with a name that describes the contents in general terms. The command is this:

mkdir (directoryname)

Then move to that directory by typing this command:

cd (directoryname)

Now type this command:

ed (nameofthefileyouwishtocreate)

Next type the letter **i**.

Type your list.

When you have finished typing, press **(ESC)** and **q**.

The asterisk will appear, whereupon you must type the letter **w**.

At the next asterisk, type the letter **q** once more. The shell prompt will return.

Create as many files as you wish under this directory.

There are many things you can do with your files once you have generated them. For instance, say you have a file that contains the names and types of locomotives on your model railroad. You would like to examine this file, or list of items.

After changing to your home directory, change again to one of the new directories you have created, by typing the letters **cd** and the name of the directory.

The shell prompt will appear once more, after which you type the letter **p**, followed by the name of the file you wish to see, like this:

p (filename)

There you are! There are the contents of your file.

UNDERSTANDING LISTS OF DIRECTORIES AND FILES

After you have created a number of files under a new directory, change to your home directory by typing **cd** plus your name. Then type the two letters **ls**.

After a few seconds, you should see a complete list of the directories and files that you have created under your name. How do you tell the difference between a directory and a file?

You will notice that some of the names have a **+** sign in front. Those are the names of the directories. All others are files.

When you type the letters **ls** while in your own directory, you will see a list of files and directories that come directly under, or that have been created directly in, that directory. You will probably think that some of the files are missing. Change directory to one of the names with a **+** sign in front by typing this:

cd (directoryname)

Now type the letters **ls** once more. Now you will see the files that have been created under *that* directory. If you did not create any files there, all you will see is the shell prompt:

%

Now change directory to herriott, the directory you generated earlier. When you have done this, type **ls** again and you will see all the files and directories you created there.

The listing of files and directories is displayed in alphabetical order. There is no means of knowing what files exist under what directories. A diagram of the files and directories under the name ''herriott'' would appear as in Figure 4.1.

The items ''books'' and ''clothes'' are files directly accessible from the user name ''herriott''. The files ''British'' and ''Canadian'' are directly under the directory ''stamps''.

If you type the command **cd stamps** and then the letters **ls** (when the shell prompt % appears, of course!), you will see just the files ''British'' and ''Canadian''.

RELEASING DIRECTORIES AND FILES

I promised that you would get rid of these directories and files (unless, of course, you wish to hold them as a pattern for the future), and you will do that right now.

After the % prompt, type this:

frel books

Next:

frel clothes

Next, change directory to stamps (**cd stamps**) and then type these commands:

frel British
frel Canadian

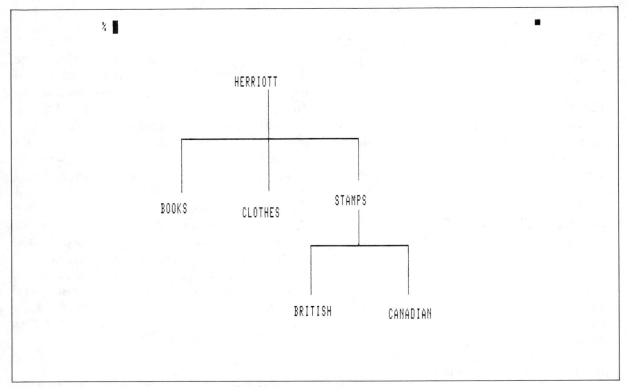

Figure 4.1   The files and directories under the name "herriott".

Now you can get rid of the directories. The command **frel** stands for "files release". The command to release directories is equally sensible — **drel**, or directory release.

So —:

drel stamps

Before you can release a directory, you must release the files inside it. Just imagine if you were to give up some space in the warehouse without moving all your stuff out first!

Now you can get rid of that herriott chap:

drel herriott

At last!

FILING PROGRAMS

Now you are going to write a short program in BASIC. You will see why in a second or two.

Change to your home directory once more by typing the letters **cd** followed by your name. When you see the shell prompt, type this:

basic

That stands for Waterloo BASIC, the variety the ICON understands. You will have to wait for a little while and may think nothing is happening. However, if you look up at the top right corner of your screen, you will see a flashing square. This tells you that something is indeed happening. BASIC is being loaded. If you can see the fileserver, you will note that the square light on the front is also flashing while the language loads into your ICON.

Eventually a message will announce that BASIC has been loaded and indicate the number of bytes free. The word **READY** will also appear. The ICON sits there waiting for your instructions.

Type the following (very carefully if you are unfamiliar with Waterloo BASIC):

---

10 print ''What is your name please?''
20 input a$
30 print ''Hello'', a$
40 print ''I am your ICON''
50 end

Not a remarkable program, by any means. Run the program by typing the word **run** or just the letter **r**. Enter your name and watch the response the computer makes.

The word **READY** will appear once more, after which you can type the word **list** or just the letter **l**. The program listing will appear on the screen once more.

Now type this:
save hello
The ICON will work away for a while and then inform you of the save. (You are not going into too much detail on BASIC at this point because I have another purpose in mind.)

Now type the word **bye**.

You have exited BASIC and are now back in the main system.

Type the letters **wmi**, and the computer should indicate that you are in your home directory.

After the shell prompt, type **ls**.

Among the files that you generated earlier, you will find one called ''hello''. You see! Programs can also be files and can be called up quite simply. It is a good idea to label a BASIC program with a name such as ''hello.bas'' — complete with period. Then you will know that that particular file is a program. For programs in Pascal, you would place a period and the letters ''pas'' after the program name as follows:

hello.pas

In this way, you can distinguish all your files from one another.

A much better way to arrange programs in various languages is to keep them together under specific directories. If you are writing a lot of BASIC programs, create a directory called ''basic''. Put all your BASIC programs there, but still label them with ''.bas'' just so that you can be certain of what they are. Likewise with Pascal, Logo, and C programs. Text files can be organized under a text directory and each name appended with ''.txt''. The ICON is a very logical device allowing you to store things quite tidily. A regular pattern for organizing files and directories will help your work immensely.

SUMMARY

The QNX operating system manages the workings of the ICON system. It allows (or causes) the user to arrange files in a tree-like structure. Files are contained in, or under, directories. The files of one directory are not accessible from another directory. Directories may contain subdirectories, which, in turn, may contain more files.

Users can create a directory with the command **mkdir (directoryname)** and move to that directory with the command **cd (directoryname)**. Files are created and edited with the command **ed (filename)**.

Users can get rid of, or release, files with the command **frel (filename)**. Directories are released with the command **drel (directory name)**. A directory cannot be released until all the files within it have been released.

Files are also created when programs in languages such as BASIC, Logo, Pascal, and C are generated. It is wise to store all the programs in a particular language together in a directory whose name is the name of that language.

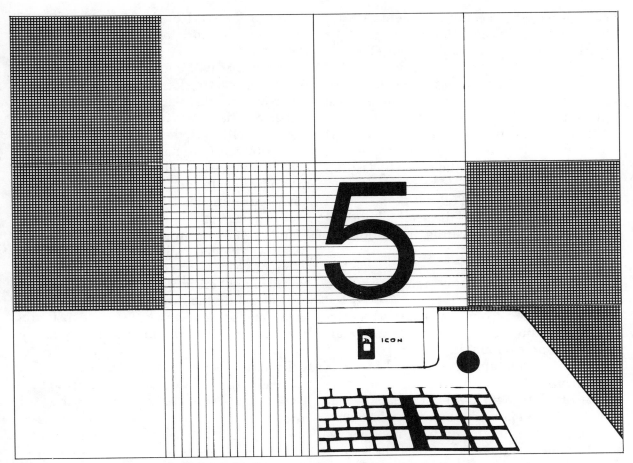

MORE FEATURES OF THE QNX

SORTING AND COPYING FILES

Let us say that you have just input a whole pile of names and addresses, wish to keep them in the order you have entered them, but also want to have an alphabetized version for printing or some other purpose without having to issue too many commands.

For instance, recently I needed a list of piano teachers in my city. I was supplied with a penciled list that was not in alphabetical order. I merely typed the names and addresses on the ICON keyboard using the copy utility. The command was this:

copy)address

The result was a neat but randomly organized list. What I needed was an alphabetized list that I could call up directly. The command was not difficult to work out. I had called my file "address". I wished to call the final, alphabetized result "pianoteachers". The command was as follows:

sort address)pianoteachers⟨ENTER⟩

Quite simply, this command says: Sort the contents of the file "address" into alphabetical order and send the result to the new file "pianoteachers".

The process was complete in a very short time — literally a couple of seconds — and then I was able to verify the result by issuing this command:

p pianoteachers⟨ENTER⟩

Because I did not need the original file any more, I erased it by issuing the following command:

frel address⟨ENTER⟩

This means, as you know, release the file called "address".

Because I had a printer attached to my fileserver, I could then issue this command:

print pianoteachers⟨ENTER⟩

The result was an alphabetized list in *hard-copy* form — that is, printed on paper.

The problem with hard-copy lists is that they tend to remain as they were when they were printed, or to end up with new names scribbled all over them. The ICON allows you to add names to your list at any time. Let us say that I discover a few piano teachers whom I did not previously know about, and I want to insert them in alphabetical order; it would be very inconvenient if I had to type out a new list. Likewise if a teacher left town and had to be removed from the list. The command to add items to a list, or, as we say in computerese, "append items to a file", is this:

copy))pianoteachers

Note that the **))** symbol is really the **)** symbol pressed twice. *Do not use the* **))** *symbol*

found to the right of the right-hand SHIFT key, because that is one of the French symbols!

The cursor will set itself below the shell prompt %, waiting for your input. Merely add the names and then press ∧**d** when you have finished. The result will be a bit mixed up; first you will have the original alphabetized list, with the new names at the end in the order in which you entered them. Just issue the command to sort, as before, and you will have your new list.

Now, although you went to the trouble of deleting your original file, which you will recall was named "address", you can see the value of keeping the data or items in "raw" form somewhere in your system. The business of taking the raw data, calling it a new name, and sorting it is a little time-consuming but was used to demonstrate a multiple command.

There is a better and quicker way.

Create a file called "towns" using the **copy)** command. The screen will appear as follows:

---

copy)towns
St. John's
Vancouver
Washington
London
Berlin
Prague
Ottawa
Toronto
Sydney
Perth
Rome

Moscow
(Add any city and town names you wish.)
%

Now you have a file called "towns". You can take the data from that file and use it as the input to another file or as the source material upon which you wish to work. Do the latter first, by sorting the contents of the file.

sort towns

The result is the alphabetized list, as you might expect. If you expand the command just a little to include a new symbol, you can store the alphabetized result directly. You are going to have to type all the names of the cities once more, but first issue this command:

copy ¦sort)cities

The new symbol is ¦, which can be found on the key directly to the right of the RUBOUT key, which is to the right of the space bar. Type the command in carefully, leaving spaces in the correct places.

Now the ICON is ready to accept your input. You can type in whatever city names take your fancy. Type ∧d when you have finished.

The shell prompt is returned, and you can then type **p cities** to see the alphabetized list.

What is that new symbol? It is the piping symbol ¦. PIP is a command found in another operating system, called CP/M. The letters stand for "peripheral interchange program", which is a long-winded way of saying "copy". You see, even files are regarded by the ICON as individual *devices*, or parts of the system. That approach makes it easy to shift or copy data from one file to another, or to use data from one file as the input for another or the output for another, in much the same way that books can be moved from a bookshelf (storage) to a desk or your hand for use.

In Chapter 9, you will be shown a means of sending the output or result of the workings of a BASIC program to a file. The contents of the new file can then be used by the operating system as the input to yet another file without your having to resort to complex programming in any of the languages. The operating system is like another language, allowing you great facility in data manipulation.

MOVING BETWEEN DIRECTORIES

In this section, you are going to create your own "tree" of directories and files, examine the result, and move between the various branches. You will recall how a small tree was created in the preceding chapter with one branch dealing only with stamps. The "stamps" branch had two subsidiary branches. The tree structure about to be created is an expansion of the fundamental concept of the hierarchical tree structure on which the QNX operating system is based.

First of all, make sure that you are in your home directory by typing this command:

wmi

The response on the screen should look like this:

%/user/(yourname)
%

If it does not, merely type this command:

cd⟨ENTER⟩

As soon as you have the correct response on the screen, type this command:

mkdir directory⟨ENTER⟩

Although it may seem a little silly, what you are going to do with this command is create a new directory called "directory".

As soon as the shell prompt is returned to you, type this command:

cd directory⟨ENTER⟩

Now type this command:

wmi

This response should appear on the screen:

/user/(yourname)/directory

Now type a new command:

mkdir subdirectory⟨ENTER⟩

Then type this command:

cd subdirectory⟨ENTER⟩

When you type the command **wmi** this time, the screen should respond with this legend:

/user/(yourname)/directory/subdirectory

One more time! Type this command:

mkdir subsubdirectory⟨ENTER⟩

When the shell prompt is returned to you, type the command to change to the new directory (**cd subsubdirectory**).

Now type **wmi** once more. The screen will respond with a long string of names separated by slashes, thus:

/user/(yourname)/directory/subdirectory/
subsubdirectory

All of the responses to the command **wmi** were path names. A *path name* is a collection of names that shows the path along a particular branch of the tree structure of directories and files. Longer paths, of course, are indicated by longer path names. Each directory in a path name can contain files of any type, whether programs in a particular language, or data or text files created through the copy, sort, or edit utilities, as described earlier.

First of all, you created a new directory in your home, or user, directory, followed by a new directory in that one, followed by yet another new directory in that one. Each directory is a discrete area that can contain whatever you wish. Files in one directory cannot be directly accessed from another. You must first change to the directory that contains the files you wish to examine or use.

Having put yourself in the deepest level that you have so far created, you will work your way back up to your home directory.

Type this command:

cd ∧⟨ENTER⟩

The ∧ symbol is the same as that used for CONTROL when typing a ∧**c** command and is, of course, found above the numeral 6 on the top of the QWERTY keyboard. In this case, the command **cd ∧** (don't forget the space!) means: "change up one level in the structure". If you now type the command

wmi⟨ENTER⟩

you will see that one of the items, the last one, in the path name has now disappeared. Type the **cd ∧** command once more to see the next item disappear. You should now see this path name:

/user/(yourname)/directory

Type the **cd ∧** command once more. You are back in your home directory.

So far, so good. You can create directories and move through them by steps, backwards and forwards. What if you are in your home directory and wish to move directly to the last directory in the tree? You can simply type the entire path name (you have to know it, of course!). In this case, you type the following:

**cd /user/(yourname)/directory/subdirectory
/subsubdirectory**

It is important to type the first part, **/user/
(yourname)**, before you type the remainder, or else you will see the chilling message cd failed.

To return directly to your home directory, you simply type this:

cd⟨ENTER⟩

Note that the caret (∧) is not used.

"Ah!" you'll say. "What if I cannot recall the whole path name in one shot?"

Well, the ICON has a very useful program that displays, among other things, the whole path name for you. That program is the subject of the next section.

Using the Visual Change Directory

Type the command **cd** to return to your home directory if you have not already done so. Now type this command:

vcd⟨ENTER⟩

The letters **vcd** stand for "visual change directory".

On the screen, you will see a design similar to the one in Figure 5-1. There will be three rectangles, the top one of which contains a slash /; the second contains the word user, and the third contains your name. Underneath these there will be a group of lines, rather like a family tree. There will be seven lines hanging down. If you have seven files and/or directories emanating from your

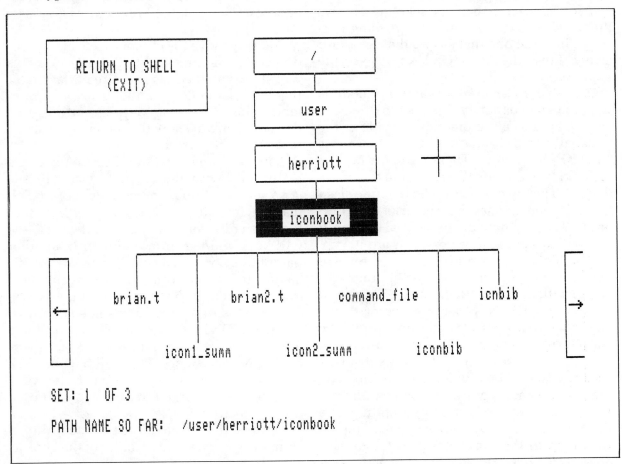

Figure 5.1 One user's "family tree" of directories and files, called up with the **vcd** command.

home directory, then there will be labels next to each line. If you have six or fewer files, there will be one or more lines without labels. Labels enclosed in rectangles indicate directories. Labels without rectangles are file names. Should you have more than seven directories or files in your home directory, then the display will tell you that you are looking at 1 of *n* sets. This information can be found to the left of the display. The bottom line shows the path name so far. It should be showing /user/(yourname).

If you have more than one set of files, move the trackball pointer over to the rectangle on the right — the one that shows the rightward arrow. Press the **(ACTION)** key to see the next frame.

One of the frames will show a rectangle with the label **directory**. This is the directory you created a few moments ago. Move the trackball cursor to that rectangle, and press **(ACTION)** as before. There will now be four rectangles in a vertical array at the top of the display. The top one shows the root (the slash /), the second one has the label **user**, the third one will show your login name, and the fourth one will show the directory you are in currently. This one is highlighted in reverse mode. Beneath it you will see another rectangle with the label **subdirectory**. There will be no other labels. Move the cursor to the new **subdirectory** rectangle, and press the **(ACTION)** key once more. The screen will change, this time to show the new subsubdirectory. Take a look at the path name. You can see that each stage of the name indicates a particular level of directory depth. Move back through the directories by bringing the cursor up to the highlighted rectangle and pressing **(ACTION)**. Note how the path name changes, deleting one level. Work your way

back to your home directory, making a note of the fact that, if there are no directories or files present, the display will warn you of that.

You can use the vcd utility to look at other files, too — but not their contents!

Move the cursor to the rectangle labeled **user**, and press the **(ACTION)** key. Now you will see a frame of rectangles, each with the name of a user. The names **demo** and **icon** will be common to all systems (at least for the time being). The other names will depend on who is signed on your system as a user.

You may move the cursor to one of the user directories and press the **(ACTION)** key. This will show you the files and directories under that user name. You cannot access the contents of any file from vcd. The utility was designed only to show the hierarchical structure of the file system.

Now move the cursor to the root rectangle — the one with the slash /. You will see a variety of things here, some of which may be meaningless to you, but you will find such directories as **config** and **util**. (These will be examined in more detail in another part of this book.) One of the directories will be labeled **user**. You will probably have to work through the frames (by moving the cursor to the right-arrow rectangle and pressing **(ACTION)**) to find it. When you have found it, move the cursor over it, and press **(ACTION)** once more. This will put you back in the user directory. Now you can find your own login name and move back to your own home directory.

I suggest that you explore the vcd utility at your leisure, using this section of the book as a guide.

When you exit from the utility, by moving

the cursor to the **RETURN TO SHELL** rectangle, you will see the last path name displayed on the screen. Now you can see how the vcd utility serves a double purpose: to demonstrate the tree structure of files and directories and to indicate the path name so that you can move directly to a particular spot in your structure.

Merely type in exactly what you see on the top of the screen under **PATH NAME OF LAST DISPLAYED DIRECTORY**: and there you are!

EXPLORING THE ROOT OF THE TREE

The great advantage of an operating system like QNX is that everything is there for you to see and discover, if you know how!

You will have noticed that each item of every path name is separated by a slash /. Indeed, the path name begins with a slash. The slash represents the root of the tree, the beginning of the hierarchical structure of files and directories. It is possible to see each stage of the structure by issuing the appropriate commands. To move to the root of the structure, you must type this command:

cd /

The shell prompt will return, and then you may type this command:

ls

You will note that there is a variety of directories and files under the root. You will probably have examined the list using the vcd utility.

You can examine any of the contents of the directories by typing the **cd** followed by the relevant directory name. For example:

cd /rel_1.13_info

This will place you in the directory that contains information on the 1.13 version of the operating system. (If you have version 2.0 or 2.1, the file will, of course, indicate that.) To see the files contained in that directory, type this:

p (filename)

Some of the information may well appear complex, yet you will find a great deal that is of interest as you progress.

Change directory up one level, by issuing this command:

cd ∧

Now issue this command:

cd /cmds

If you forget to type in the slash, you will receive the message cd failed.

The command **ls** will show the contents of this directory. Some of the contents will appear familiar, and they should, for they are the very same commands you have been using to control the ICON.

The commands **copy**, **sort**, **files**, and **mkdir** you have already used. No doubt you have made extensive use of the **p** command. The commands **frel** and **drel** were covered in Chapter 4. It appears as if some of the commands are missing! Change directory to the lib by issuing this command:

cd /lib

In the library, you will find things that look after other things. That isn't a very scientific explanation, I know, but the contents of the lib look after a variety of activities, some of them very small, that allow you to control the ICON.

Change to the icons directory. Now show the sorted list by typing **ls**.

As you would expect from the directory name, this is where all the icons that you see on the screen are kept. If you print one of them to the screen by issuing the command

p briefcase

you will see several rows of figures, most of them zeros. This is the way the ICON stores all the bits and pieces in its memory. It is in code, of course, and the code has a name: "hex-code", short for "hexadecimal code". This is a method of counting by sixteens rather than by tens; but that is a topic for another book!

Change back to the root and examine another directory, this time the spool. When you issue the **ls** command, you will see two new directories: parallel and serial. You probably know that there are two major forms of allowing a computer to talk to such things as printers and other computers. The words serial and parallel refer to these two forms. In the former, messages go down the cable from the computer to the printer, and then messages go back from the printer to the computer to say that the computer's message has been received and understood and is being acted upon. In the parallel type of interface, the messages pass backwards and forwards at one and the same time.

If you change to one of these directories (no slash needed this time), you will see just the shell prompt, indicating that there are no files there. If you find sets of numbers in either of these directories, then there is something wrong. You are likely to get some very strange things on your precious printer paper!

Spooling refers to the ability of the ICON to keep everyone's printing jobs separate, saving a lot of headaches sorting out which words belong to whose work! Spooling also refers to the ability of the ICON to store the work to be printed in a special spot so that you can go on and produce some new work while printing is in progress.

Under the root (change back to the root directory), you will find the config and util directories. The word config refers to "configuration", or organization; util refers to the various utilities or fixed programs that perform a variety of tasks for you. Here you will find such goodies as ied, the icon editor; ui, the user interface; and vcd, the visual change directory utility, which you have been exploring recently.

The attach and detach utilities are for setting up the ICON system when it first arrives, or when new user stations are added.

Play with the **echo** command for a moment or two. Just type **echo**. The cursor will sit under the command and appear to do nothing. As with the **copy** command, the ICON is waiting for you to type something on the keyboard. No sooner have you pressed **(ENTER)** than the screen "echoes" what you have typed. To exit, type ∧**d** as with the **copy** command.

The command **park** might seem odd. It is used when the system is to be dismantled and transported somewhere. The **park** command sets the heads in the disk drive in a special position, rather like the park setting on an automobile gearshift. As a result, the fileserver hard disk is relatively safe from jolts and knocks. The file rmt_park does the same for the floppy disk drive.

Return to the root directory to look at one more thing.

While in the cmds directory, you may have noticed a command called **cat**. This stands for "concatenate", which means "string together". You will use the **cat** command when you deal with the graphics editor. For the moment, issue this command:

cat owl.t

Then watch the screen. When you have finished, type a new **cat** command, but this time with the modifier (anything that follows a command is a modifier) **figure.t**. When the graphics editor is introduced (Chapter 7), you will have a chance to produce your own masterpieces.

The command

cat

can also be used just like the **copy** command. Issue it, and the screen will wait for you to type in a few items. To get out of the cat mode, you must type ∧**d**.

THE USER INTERFACE

(Note: The following description may not be accurate for the version of the user interface that you have; the principles, however, will be the same. See ''Note'' in Preface.)

The word *interface* is an example of computer jargon. It is the name given to the means of allowing two otherwise quite separate devices to talk to each other.

A computer cannot talk to a printer without the correct form of interface. It is the interface that translates what the computer has to say into language the printer can understand. Having understood, the printer can then carry out the computer's commands.

A piano has an interface between the player and the strings: the keyboard. The keyboard is a standard device consisting of wooden levers covered in some material, usually white for the flat ones and black for the raised ones, which translate or transform the finger motion of the player into hammer strokes.

An automobile has a number of interfaces: there is a pedal that translates foot pressure into gasoline flow, another that translates foot pressure into braking action, a lever that releases the door lock, and so on.

An ordinary light switch is an interface.

Returning to the musical analogy for a moment, the notes on the page are an interface between the composer and the player. The composer uses commonly understood symbols to communicate ''sound thoughts''. The player then translates these symbols into physical actions appropriate to the instrument he or she is playing.

The ICON system provides a means of moving around the system without having to know a great deal about commands: the user interface. The interface is very advanced, yet using it is almost as simple as pointing at pictures.

The usual manner of human-computer interfacing is via the keyboard. The user interface on the ICON system, however, makes extensive use of the trackball.

Place yourself in your home directory and then type this command:

ui

After a few moments, you will see on the screen something that resembles Figure 5.2. The layout looks similar to that of the text editor, which you will meet in Chapter 6. In fact, some of the symbols—the scissors, paste pot, camera, and glasses — are the same. At the top of the screen, there are symbols, or icons, on either side of the directory name. The directory name is in this form:

1:/user/(loginname)

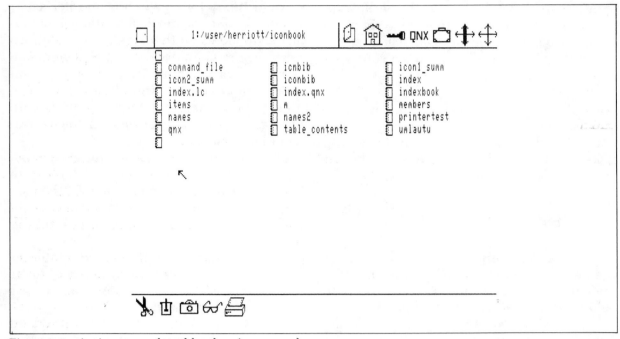

Figure 5.2   An image produced by the **ui** command.
The doors represent the directories in the user's home
directory.

The numeral 1: indicates that you are accessing the files from the hard disk. If you
were accessing material from the floppy disk,
the numeral would be 2:. To the right of the
path or directory name, there is an open door
and then a house. The house represents your
home directory. The key to the right of the
house is the way out of the user interface.
You will deal with the remainder of the icons
as you work your way through the user
interface.

Beneath the top row of icons, there will be
some doors. The number of doors will be the
same as the number of directories that exist
in your home directory, plus one. The extra
one is blank and is there to allow you to create a new directory.

Beneath the row of directory doors, there
will be a row of notebooks. The number of
notebooks will correspond to the number of
files in your home directory, plus one. The
extra notebook, like the extra directory door,
is there to let you create a new file in your
home directory.

One of your directories will be called **directory**. You created it using the **mkdir** command in direct QNX mode, you will recall.
Bring the arrow or cursor over the door
marked **directory**, and press the **⟨ACTION⟩**
key. The display will change to show the directory "underneath", or "within", the directory marked **directory**. Again there will be
one extra, blank door. There will also be a
blank notebook. Move the cursor to the

subdirectory door and press the **(ACTION)** key. Now you have the new display showing the subdirectory together with a blank directory door and a blank file notebook.

Note how the path name changes to reflect the levels you have moved through.

Bring the cursor to the right of the blank file notebook, and type this command:

file1

If nothing happens, just move the cursor a shade to the right and try again. No sooner do you type the first letter than a window opens with the legend new file name.

When you have finished typing the new file name, press the **(ACTION)** key. Do not press **(ENTER)**, for nothing will happen if you do.

The activity rectangle, a small reverse image in the right top corner, will blink for a moment or two, and then the display will change. The new file name will appear next to a notebook, in the correct alphabetical position, and a fresh, blank file notebook will be waiting.

Create files 2 and 3 in the same manner.

Now move the cursor to the open-door icon to the left of the house. The display will change to show that you have now moved up one level to the subdirectory. The open door is the equivalent of typing **cd** ∧. You will notice that the path name has been reduced to reflect the fact that "subdirectory" is to be found in the "directory" directly beneath your home directory.

Bring the cursor to the blank directory door and type this command:

subdirectory1

Press the **(ACTION)** key when you have finished. The new directory name will appear alongside the hitherto blank door, and a new blank door will appear. Create a file in the file "notebook", and call it "file1" as before.

Now move your cursor to the subdirectory1 door, and press **(ACTION)**. The display will change to show that there are no directories or files there. Create a new directory and also a new file. Call the directory "subdirect1". If you call it "subdirectory1", you may become confused.

Create yet another directory, called "subdirect2", and then create your new file. The path name shown at the top will be this:

1:/user/(yourname)/directory/subdirectory1

Quite a rats' nest of directories you are creating!

Move the cursor to the open door, and the display will change. Work your way back to your home directory, and then explore for a little while, moving back and forth through the directories. When you have reached the end of the line, and a long path name is being displayed, move the cursor to the house icon, and then press **(ACTION)**. Immediately you will find yourself back at your home directory. The house icon is the equivalent of typing the command **cd** without the caret.

Work your way down through the directories once more, stopping at your convenience where there is a set of files. Choose one of the files and bring the cursor over the notebook itself — not alongside as before. Press the **(ACTION)** key.

The display will change, the principal differences being that the bottom row of icons will have disappeared, as will the open door, the house, the key, and the letters QNX. The cursor will be somewhere up in the top left corner. Type a few words, such as these:

This is file1

Then bring the cursor up to the notebook icon in the top left corner, and press the

(ACTION) key. When the activity rectangle stops blinking, move the cursor to the door to the right of the pencil, and press the (ACTION) key once more. Now you are back in the user interface. Bring the cursor back to file1, and press the (ACTION) key. You are back to the file, and the words you have just typed are back on the screen. Go to the door and press (ACTION). Now you are back in the user interface mode.

The text editor, which is where you wrote the words **This is file1**, will be dealt with later. If you wish to explore Chapter 9 now, feel free to do so, coming back to this chapter when you are ready.

Accessing Graphics Files

When you have been working with the ICON for a while, you will find among your files a number of titles, not all of which will refer to text. For example, you may have produced some pictures with the graphics editor or created some icons of your own with the icon editor.

You can access these files with the user interface, but what you see on the screen will be quite unintelligible. For the moment, it is better to confine the use of the user interface to the business of seeing what files you have and directly accessing those that are text.

Moving In and Out of the User Interface

Employing the user interface is a little like moving from room to room in a house. The first room you enter is your "home room", or home directory. To get to other rooms, you move the cursor to the directory door — one of the small doors at the top of the screen. To move back through the rooms, you move the cursor to the door next to the house icon. To move directly from whatever room you are in back to the "home room", you place the cursor on the house icon.

To exit from the user interface, you move the cursor over the key — in effect, locking your house behind you and securing all the contents. You are now outside the house.

Now, it can be a nuisance to have to lock the door every time you want to step outside to see something, so there is a means of "coming outside" — as it were, looking around in the garden, visiting next door, and chatting over the garden fence — without locking the door.

The icon you use for this is the one that consists of three letters: QNX. The letters are the name of the operating system. You can move directly to the operating system and do all the things you wish to without actually leaving your territory.

When Files Overflow Their Rooms

As your use of the ICON increases and you develop sets of files, you may find that the user interface gives you the message **room too large to see completely**. Merely press the (ACTION) key, and a portion of the contents of your "home room" will appear on the screen. To see the remainder, move the cursor to one of the sets of crossed arrows at the top right-hand corner of the screen, press (ACTION), and roll the trackball under your fingers. Now you can see the remainder of your room. For convenience, it will probably be a good plan, at least at first, to keep each of your rooms (directories) of such a size that the file names will all fit on the screen. As you progress, overflows will cause you no problems.

Transporting Files with the Briefcase

The briefcase icon has probably been intriguing you. This icon is used for "transporting" files from place to place, usually from one directory to another under your home directory, but it can be used to move files from user to user. The procedure is just as straightforward as other aspects of the user interface.

Bring the cursor next to the empty directory door, and type the word **briefcase**. Then press **⟨ACTION⟩**. After a few moments, the screen will change to reflect your addition. Note that, if you have no directory beginning with a letter "a" or "b-plus-some-other-letter-earlier-than-r", your new directory will be in the top left-hand corner. Do not look in the last spot you put the cursor at, for the listings of directories and files is immediately alphabetized!

Now select one of your files by placing the cursor over the first letter of the file name, not the notebook. Press **⟨ACTION⟩**.

The file or notebook name will be highlighted. Move the cursor to the scissors, and cut the file. It will disappear from the listing on the screen.

Move to a new directory door, and move through it by pressing **⟨ACTION⟩**.

Select an empty directory door, and type the word **briefcase** as before. Press **⟨ACTION⟩**, and a new briefcase will appear.

Now highlight the new word briefcase, and then move the cursor to the paste or glue pot. Press **⟨ACTION⟩** once more, and the new directory will now contain the file you deleted from the previous one.

Sound complicated? Step through it once more with me.

Create a directory called "new" in the directory you are now in, and then create another called "briefcase" in that same directory.

Create a file or notebook called "newone" in the directory you are currently in. Now delete it by using the scissors icon.

Next, move to your directory called "new", and move through the door. There are no files or directories in that directory. Create a directory called "briefcase".

Highlight your new briefcase, and then move the cursor to the paste pot. Press **⟨ACTION⟩**, and the file "newone" will appear under your directory called "new".

Move back up one level by placing the cursor over the open-door icon at the top of the screen (to the left of the house). Select the briefcase, and then move the cursor to the paste pot once more. The file "new" has now been replaced where it started.

You have not only moved a file from one directory to another but have also seen how to duplicate it in two directories. You will have realized that it is a simple matter just to type the names in the directories without using the briefcase. But what if the files have some contents?

Create, by means of the text editor, some contents in each of the files "newone". Make each set of contents different. Now move them around using the briefcase.

Now you can see that the briefcase facility is a means of moving not just names but whole files with their contents.

It would seem that you have a whole pile of briefcases, would it not?

That is not exactly true. The briefcase is shared, as you will see if you now move the cursor to the briefcase icon next to the QNX in the top right corner. You can see that your

47

briefcase contains all of the files you moved and is becoming quite bulky. Whether you leave them there is up to you and depends on how much manipulation you wish to perform on those files.

Notice that the briefcase icon has now disappeared, and in its place there is a door. This is the way to get out of your briefcase. (I suppose the designers would have found it difficult to produce a graphic image of the inside of a briefcase!) In any case, the door icon is a standard symbol on the ICON system to indicate the "way out".

SUMMARY

In this chapter, more of the utilities of the QNX operating system were explored.

The operating system allows material to be read directly from the keyboard, copied to another file, sorted, and then sent to yet another file. Material can be kept in both raw and processed forms. Material can be added to a file without the original contents' being disturbed. The new contents can be sorted with the old to create yet another file.

The **p** command sends material to the screen. The **print** command sends material to the printer, which produces a hard copy.

The creation of directories and files produces a path name that is at once a description of the route through the tree structure and a means of direct access to a particular file without the repetitious issuing of many commands.

The vcd program displays the tree structure of files and directories and indicates the path name. The utilities themselves are stored in the "root" of the tree and can be reached by the command **cd /**.

The ICON system takes its name from the icons, or symbols, that often stand for complicated sets of commands. The icons in the user interface allow users to create and move files and directories with ease.

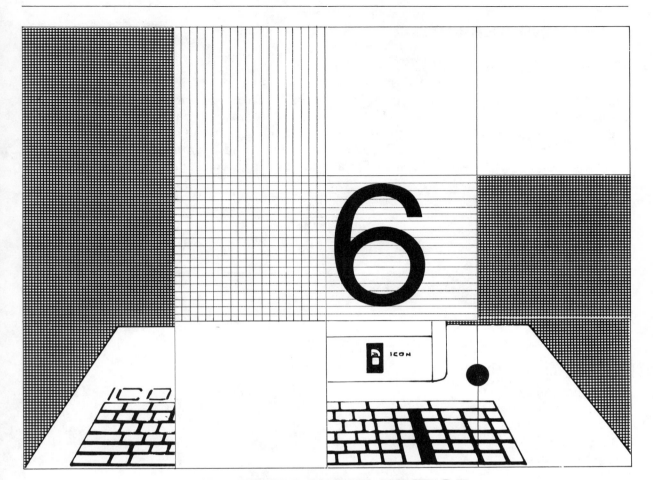

THE ICON TEXT EDITOR

In Chapter 5, you were introduced to the icons, or symbols, from which the ICON system gets its name. The icons represented particular types of action that you could take in the user interface mode in order to store, retrieve, and transport information.

As you learn to use the text editor, you will recognize some of the same symbols, and meet some new ones. In this chapter, you will learn how to put a piece of your writing — a term paper, perhaps — on the screen, revise it there, and print out a perfect copy.

USING THE EDITOR

Meeting the Editor

Type the following after the shell prompt %:
  edit test
Then wait a few moments. Shortly, the screen will change to look like Figure 6.1. The center of the screen will be blank, save for a solitary arrow. At the top left corner of the screen, there will be a notebook, then the name of the file you are working on, in this case **test**, and then a pencil, a door, clipboards, and two sets of NSEW arrows.

Figure 6.1 The image produced by the **edit test** command.

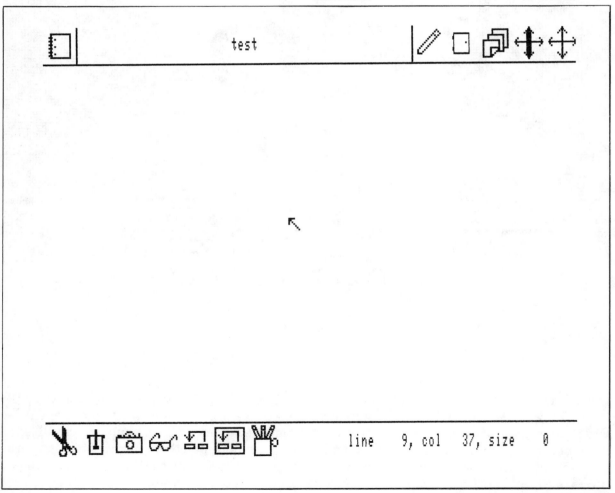

At the bottom of the screen, you can see scissors, a paste pot, a camera, glasses, two strange objects, and a mug full of pencils. To the right of these icons, you will see the status line — a line that tells which line and column the arrow is sitting on in the page or screen you are working on. (Each line on a computer screen has 80 places for characters. There are normally 25 lines on a screen. The character places line up vertically. Computerists refer to these vertical lineups as columns.)

Move the arrow by gently rolling the trackball under the fingers of your right hand. Do not use the palm of your hand, or you will never achieve the fine control necessary for the speedy and precise work you are going to do in this and later chapters. Keep the thumb of your right hand over the ACTION key on the right. Or, if you prefer, you can use the ACTION key on the left; the two keys perform the same function. Place the arrow just a little way down the screen.

Typing on the Screen

Let's explore the editor—for that is what you are working with now—by first typing something on the screen. Try the following if you cannot think of anything grand to say:

This is the ICON text editor, and I am going to explore it for the first time.

As you type, you will notice that the arrow moves with the letters as they appear on the screen, rather the way small children point to the letters as they are reading. The status line also changes, showing the number of the column on which the arrow is now resting. Do not let the number go any higher than about 76, for the present; press the

(ENTER) key at around that figure. The arrow will move to the beginning of the next line. So far everything is just like a typewriter.

Correcting Mistakes

In order to learn how to correct mistakes, you have to make a mistake. For the purposes of demonstration, type the sentence I suggested in the preceding section, and put an extra letter ''p'' in ''explore''.

Move the arrow (using the trackball) until it is over the second ''p''. Now find the key with the leftward-pointing arrow. It is just to the left of the RESET key on the top row of the QWERTY keyboard. Press the left-arrow key once. The extra ''p'' will disappear, and the remainder of the line will move to the left. Just to make sure you know which letter is removed when you press the left-arrow key, do it once more. This time it will be the ''x'' that is removed.

Leave the arrow where it is, and just type the letter ''x''. The ''x'' is put back in place.

From now on, I am going to refer to the left-arrow key as the DELETE key. Do not confuse it with the RUBOUT key at the bottom of the keyboard.

Carry on typing, remembering to press **(ENTER)** at the end of each line when the column number is around 76. You will notice that the line number increases as you type new lines. So does the size number. In fact, for the moment, line and size numbers are identical. Press **(ENTER)** at the end of the next line you type, and then press it again. A blank line will appear on your screen. If you compare line and size numbers now, you will notice that size is greater than line. The line number is the actual number of lines of text or writing. The size number is the number of lines *plus* any blank lines you have inserted.

Removing and Replacing Parts of Text

Let us say that you wish to cut out a section of your typing. It is fairly clear that the scissors might have something to do with such an activity.

First, bring the arrow over the first letter of the word or words you wish to remove. Then, keeping your thumb pressed on the **(ACTION)** key, move the trackball so that the word or words are highlighted in reverse on the screen. If you produce a large bar of amber highlighting, do not worry. The trackball will take just a little getting used to, but patience will help. When you reach the end of the word or words, release the **(ACTION)** key. The letters will stay highlighted.

Now bring the arrow down to the bottom left corner, and place it over the scissors. They will now appear in reverse. Now press the **(ACTION)** key and release it.

Presto! The words have disappeared! Don't worry. They are stored away somewhere, and you will find them in a moment or two.

Let us say that you wish to put the same words that you have just cut somewhere else on the screen. Bring the arrow to some point on the screen — it doesn't matter where — and then press the **(ACTION)** key. A small amber rectangle will appear in that spot. The place is marked.

Now bring the arrow down to the paste pot (next to the scissors), and, when it is highlighted, press **(ACTION)**. The recently removed words will now appear in that spot on the screen.

Now try putting them back where they were. Remember to do the following, in the order shown:

1. Mark the text to be removed by bringing the cursor (the arrow) over the beginning and wiping through all the words. Press the **(ACTION)** key while you do this.

2. Bring the arrow to the scissors icon and then press **(ACTION)**.

3. Move the arrow to the new spot and press **(ACTION)**, leaving an amber rectangle there.

4. Move the arrow to the paste-pot icon and then press **(ACTION)**.

Always mark the text to be modified before attempting any modification.

What if you forget to mark the text first? The ICON text editor will let you know that you must mark the text first. Try bringing the arrow to the scissors without marking any text. Press the **(ACTION)** key and see what happens. You see? It tells you that no text has been selected to be cut. Likewise with the paste pot.

Adding Headings

Perhaps you would like to type a heading above your text. Bring the cursor (the arrow) up above your work, and press the **(ENTER)** key a few times.

Now that you have some space opened up, bring the arrow back to the top of the screen at the extreme left, and begin typing. If you wish to put the heading in upper case, press down the small key just to the left of the space bar. It is the one marked CAP LOCK. The little red light will come on, warning you that everything you type now will come out in upper case — but only the alphabet keys are affected. The number and other symbol keys require the ordinary SHIFT key in order to be accessed.

Now type your heading.

THIS IS THE HEADING

Bring the cursor to the beginning of the letter "T" (or whatever happens to be the first letter of your heading), and then press the **(ACTION)** key. The letter is now marked. Do not bother to mark the remainder of the heading; the first letter is enough.

Now bring the cursor down to the pot with all the pencils in it, and press the **(ACTION)** key, keeping it down.

A window will appear showing a variety of activities that can be performed by this icon. One of the activities is already highlighted — the top one, which is do nothing, as in Figure 6.2. Holding down the **(ACTION)** key, move the trackball down gently so that the next action is highlighted. This one is centre.

Figure 6.2 The image produced by activating the pencil-pot icon. The box, or "window", shows the activities that this icon can perform.

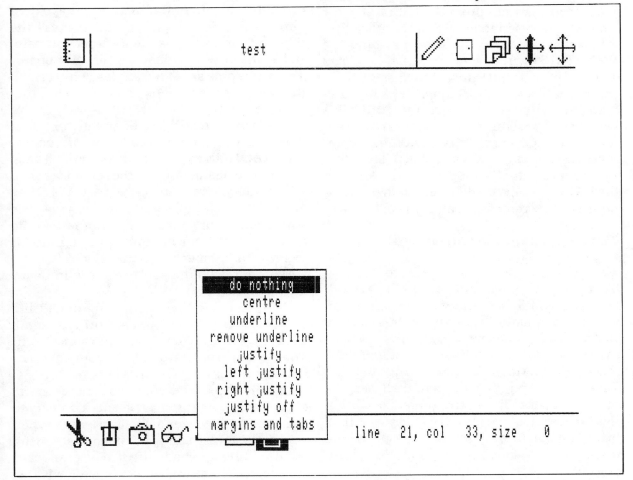

Let go of the **(ACTION)** key.

Immediately the heading you have just typed is moved rightward across the screen. It has been centered.

Now, you may argue with me, for it looks as if the heading has been pushed too far over to the right, and with respect to what you have been doing that is perfectly correct. The editor is set to deal with more than the 76 characters I suggested at the beginning. If you wish to center the heading over your work, bring the cursor up to the beginning of your heading; then press the **(DELETE)** key (the one you used to get rid of the extra "p" when you started out). Keep pressing the **(DELETE)** key until you are satisfied. If you go too far back, just press the space bar instead, and the heading will move to the right.

Incidentally, you can use the **(DELETE)** key to produce continuous deletion by keeping your finger on it. It is a feature of computers that there is always a small delay before repeat keys actually repeat. All the keys on the ICON can repeat, although on many computers only certain keys can perform this feat.

Using the Clip-board

Mark a portion of your text as before by bringing the cursor (I will not call it the "arrow" anymore) to the beginning of the words and then wiping carefully with the trackball so that a fair bit of the text is highlighted. Let us say that there are two lines of text you wish to highlight. Move the cursor from the first letter, down and then along to the last letter of the sentence. The entire sentence is highlighted. Let go of the **(ACTION)** key, and then bring the cursor down to the scissors. Press the **(ACTION)** key, and the text will disappear.

Where has it gone?

Bring the cursor up to the clip-board icon, just to the right of the door and to the left of the direction (scrolling) arrows at the top of the screen. Press **(ACTION)**.

Your text will disappear from the screen, and the title at the top, which up to now has been showing test, will show the word clip_board. Note the underscore instead of the hyphen in clip_board.

In the space where, up to now, you have been typing your text, you can see, among other things, the sentence you have just clipped out. It is highlighted, whereas the other bits are not. It is the most recent material to have been added to the clip_board. There are some small rectangles, which show the limits of the various bits and pieces that have been cut.

The cursor should still be in the same spot it was in when you moved to the clip_board. Press **(ACTION)** again, and you will be back in your text again. Replace the sentence somewhere on the screen using the paste pot. Now go back to the clip_board and see what has happened. Your sentence is still there in the clip_board, but it is no longer highlighted. It is a record of an action performed.

What else would you use the clip_board for?

Well, imagine that, while you are sitting there thinking about the next thing you are going to write, a new idea presents itself. You do not want to put it in your text yet, because it does not fit anywhere.

Use the clip_board. Keep your notes there, even whole paragraphs. It seems a bit silly to write them down on a sheet of paper when you have a vast storage device just sitting there waiting for you to use it. The clip_board allows you to store whatever you wish —

phrases, odd sentences, even terrific words that you have just discovered or do not want to forget. When you decide to use the material, you merely insert it at the appropriate spot. You can save the clip_board for the next time you work on your masterpiece.

I think the best thing you can do at this point is to play with the text editor by writing a lengthy piece, exploring all the features you have used so far. Doing this will give you a rest from reading and allow you to concentrate on what you are doing at the keyboard. When you wish to know some more or to confirm something that you have discovered by yourself, come back to this book and continue the tour with me.

Storing and Retrieving Text

One of the fundamental rules of dealing with computers, regardless of whether you are programming using one of the languages, preparing a graphic of some kind, or writing text of some sort, is to SAVE FREQUENTLY. If you are used to playing with computers, you will already know this rule.

Normally, to save something, one must type in a command such as **SAVE**, **STORE**, or **PUT**. With the ICON text editor, there is no need to type commands of any sort. Just bring the cursor up to the notebook icon at the top left corner of the screen, press **⟨ACTION⟩**, . . . and the work is saved. If you now wish to leave the editor, bring the cursor up to the door (next to the pencil at the top of the screen) and press **⟨ACTION⟩**. A small rectangle will blink rapidly on and off in the top right corner of the screen, the length of time it takes to do this depending on how long your text is and the number of people working on the system. Suddenly the screen will

blank and leave behind the familiar shell prompt %.

Type the letters **ls** and then press **⟨ENTER⟩**. Your file will appear among those listed on the screen. To return to the file, merely type this:

edit (space, filename)

and press **⟨ENTER⟩**. For example, the text you were working on was called "test", so you type the following:

edit test

After a short while, the text-editor icons will appear on the screen with the cursor in the center. Then your text will appear.

Notice that the text will show from the beginning. If you have more text than will fit on the screen, you simply move the cursor to the direction (scrolling) arrows in the top right corner. The set of arrows next to the clip-board will do just fine. Keep the cursor there and then press **⟨ACTION⟩**, rolling the trackball under your fingers so that the work scrolls up the screen. While you are in this mode, you can try scrolling to the left. The text moves in the opposite direction to that of the trackball, but the action is quite natural and should cause no difficulty. Just remember that you are really moving the cursor over the page rather than moving the page itself.

Using the Pencil Icon

Let us see what the pencil icon does.

Move the cursor up there, and then press **⟨ACTION⟩** and keep it down. You will see a group of activities displayed in the window, as shown in Figure 6.3. These are activities that you can play with on your own, later, now that you know they are there.

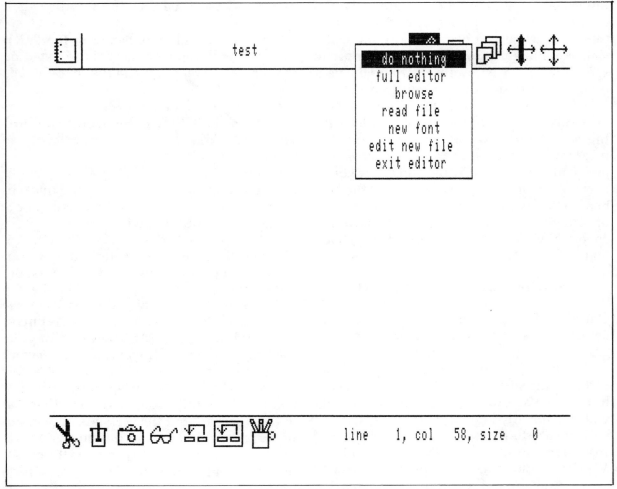

test

do nothing
full editor
browse
read file
new font
edit new file
exit editor

line   1, col   58, size   0

Figure 6.3   An image produced by activating the pencil icon.

Underlining

Now move the cursor to the pencil pot at the
bottom of the screen and press **⟨ACTION⟩**.
You have already played with the "centre"
feature. Now try the underline.

Mark a sentence as for cutting by placing the
cursor over the letters, pressing **⟨ACTION⟩**,

and moving the trackball. Let go of the
⟨ACTION⟩ key, and move the cursor to the
pencil pot. Bring the highlighting down to
the word underline and press **⟨ACTION⟩**.

There you are! The sentence is underlined.
You can remove underlining in the same way.

Simultaneous Typing and Printing

Pause here for a moment or two and ponder what this text editor that you are using really is. You must be familiar with the words *word processing*. Word processors have been around for many years. Based on computing devices, they are a means of manipulating text, recording it on some kind of magnetic medium, and then causing it to be printed out on a printer. It doesn't matter how far away the printer is from the terminal; it could even be on the moon. Some word-processing devices look very much like ordinary typewriters.

After the text has been written, most word processors require that the author or typist go through the text and insert a great number of letter codes or control codes that tell the program how the material is to be presented on the paper. It takes a long time to learn all of these codes; in fact, I do not believe that anyone can actually remember them all. Most of the time, one must look up features that are not used very often.

The ICON text editor makes such hunting unnecessary, or at least much simpler, for everything you want to know can be found right there on the screen. As you now know, in order to perform some action, you merely bring the arrow to the proper icon, press **⟨ACTION⟩**, and there you are. The screen tells you what to do. There are no complicated commands or control codes to learn.

One of the features of the ICON computer system is its ability to perform a number of activities at one and the same time. This is called *multi-tasking*, a term that is self-explanatory, really. At this moment of writing, I am using the multi-tasking feature. I wanted a printout up to and including the paragraph right before this one while I sat and thought about my work. I saved the work so far completed, left the editor, and issued the command to print by typing **print iconed** (that was the name I gave the file until I decided exactly which chapter number it would have). The file was transferred to a buffer in the fileserver, and the shell prompt % was returned to me on the screen.

Then I had a new thought. It occurred to me that I could describe what was happening, and so I returned to the text by typing **edit iconed**. The printer had not started by the time the chapter had appeared on the screen once more, but it had begun by the time I scrolled down to the end of my text!

I carried on typing, and the printer had finished printing by the time I had written the words "shell prompt" two paragraphs before this one.

The feature that allows you to print and type at the same time is a real time-saver, allowing you to get a draft of what you have done without fixing it permanently. Most microcomputers require you to wait while the printer does its work, unless you have invested in a device called a spooler, which costs extra. With the ICON, it is included.

It might interest you to know that the text, up to the point I decided to print to (the words "There are no complicated commands or control codes to learn"), was printed on five complete pages, with six more lines on a sixth. That was with single-spacing, of course. The version that goes to the publisher must be double-spaced, with wide margins.

Up to the end of this sentence, in double-spaced mode, the line number reads 544, and the size of the document, 553.

Copying Sections of Text

I expect you are extremely curious to know what the little camera icon does. Perhaps you have already brought the cursor down there and found that you were told that there was no text selected to be copied. If you have not already done that, do it now.

Now move the cursor to the top of a few sentences and then wipe down over as much as you would like. Then release the **(ACTION)** key. Now bring the cursor to the camera icon, and press **(ACTION)**. Nothing seems to happen. Unlike the scissors, the camera does not remove the selected text. Now move the cursor to a new, clear point on the screen, and press **(ACTION)** again to mark the spot.

Before you do anything, check the clip_board. Move the cursor to the clip_board, press **(ACTION)**, and then release. There is your whole section, highlighted to indicate that it is the last section to be added to the clip_board. The screen will look something like Figure 6.4.

Figure 6.4   The kind of image produced by activating the clip_board icon. The highlighted sentence was added more recently than the other sentence.

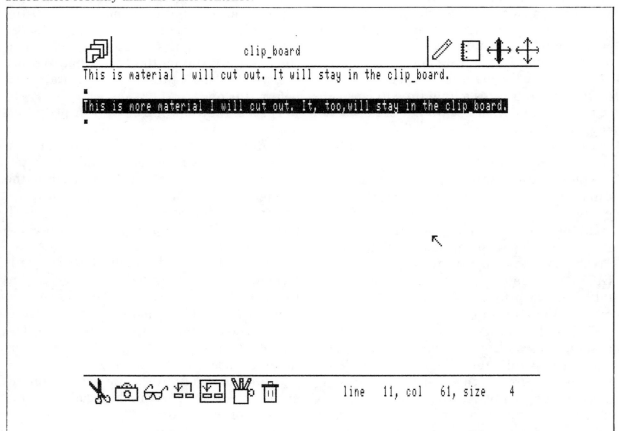

Now you have to decide where you want that material placed, and then put it there. You have already marked a spot on the screen. You will see it when you return to the editor.

Now bring the cursor down to the paste pot, and press **(ACTION)**. The whole section is now in its new spot, as well as the old. What you have done is taken a photograph or photocopy of the section and then pasted it in a new spot.

Now, if you go back to the clip_board for a moment, you will see that the material is still there. You are going to work on it in other ways.

Justifying Text

Return to the editor.

First of all, reprint the same sentences on the screen. Then mark the text by wiping through with the cursor.

Next, select the pencil-pot icon and choose the option right justify. The result will be a bit of a mess, but the letters on the right-hand side will be in one column, just the way you would see them in a book.

Then repeat the text once more, and this time, after marking it, choose the left justify option from the pencil pot. This time it is the left-hand side that will be in a column.

Repeat the text yet again, and see what happens with the justify option. This time both sides of the text will be justified, as shown in Figure 6.5. Some of the words will be spread a little far apart. Small amounts of caution and common sense are needed to use the justify feature. In order to prevent partial sentences (at the ends of paragraphs, for instance) from being spread across the page, mark only full lines. It is possible that your ICON will be able to recognize final sentences, in which case you can mark all the lines, and the text will appear perfectly normal.

Figure 6.5   A justified paragraph — the result of choosing the justify option from the pencil pot.

```
This  is a demonstration of the justification facilities on the ICON editor.
The normal fashion of producing text results in an output which has a ragged
edge,  at  least  down  one  side.  The  left  hand side usually requires no
justification for the cursor is sent as far left  as  it  can  go  when  the
<ENTER>  key is pressed. In order to justify the portion of text is selected
and then the pencil pot is addressed by the cursor. The window  appears  and
the  appropriate  justification feature is selected. For this version of the
example      the      justify      feature      has      been      selected.

    Both edges  are justified.




            JUSTIFY
```

Setting Margins

You will have noticed some of the other options in the pencil pot. One of them is called **margins and tabs**, a highly useful feature.

A typist places a sheet of paper in the machine and sets left and right margins so that there is a clear space on each side of the paper. He or she also sets tab markers so that a single press of the **(TAB)** key will move the carriage, ball, or printing element to a new spot without the typist's having to press the space bar—and perhaps overshoot the mark!

Move the cursor to the pencil pot, select **margins and tabs**, and press **(ACTION)**. A row of "t's" will appear at the bottom of the screen. Move the cursor to the left, and press the **(TAB)** key (on the left, next to Q). Set the tab so that the number 9 appears. Move the cursor over to the right, and then press the **(DELETE)** key (on the right, next to RESET). This will move the right margin to the left. Watch the column number change. Bring it down to 66. Now your text will have a reasonable margin on each side of the text, where you can put notes or editorial comments.

Automatic Search

Sometimes a writer may have misspelled a word and not caught the error immediately. Spotting another error of the same sort later on, the writer wonders whether he or she has misspelled the word that way before. Alternatively, he or she may suspect that a certain word has been overused, or that a technical term used several times was the incorrect one in certain circumstances.

How tedious it would be to have to go through the entire text word by word, looking for the errors! It is much simpler to have the computer do the job of finding the terms and replacing them with the correct versions. The principle is the same as usual: select the word you want to work on, and then select the action you wish to perform.

A word or string search automatically begins at the beginning of the text. You may, however, indicate some other point by placing the cursor at that point and marking it with the **(ACTION)** key.

Move the cursor to the glasses icon and press **(ACTION)**. Then type the text string that you wish to look for. As soon as you do this, a window will open, just like on the pencil pot. Continue typing—the string could be an entire phrase — and, when you have finished, press the **(ACTION)** key.

You will see the first instance of the desired string highlighted on the screen. Once you have found the string, decide whether you want to replace it, and, if so, move the cursor to the replace icon, which is just to the right of the glasses.

Having thought about what you wish to write instead of the string you have, begin typing. Again a window will open. When you have finished typing, press **(ACTION)**.

There you are! The old string will have disappeared, and the new string will be in its place . . . just like that!

If you want to make the same replacement repeatedly, mark the whole document. If you want to replace the string with different material each time, you must treat each instance separately as described.

Note that the glasses are to be used for looking for specific instances of something that might occur more than once. If you wish to merely replace something—a word, a phrase, or a whole paragraph — use the replace icon directly. As usual, mark the text you wish to replace by pointing at it with the cursor and wiping through the limits of the material; then point to the replace icon. Begin typing your new text, and, when you have finished, press **(ACTION)**. The deed is done!

Disposing of Garbage

Now let us return to the clip_board for a moment. In the clip_board, you find all the little bits and pieces that have been cut, pasted, copied, or whatever. Although some of this material may well be useful for another session, much of it will be garbage. And where does one put garbage? Right down there at the bottom . . . in the garbage can!

Mark the stuff you do not want, and then point to the trash can with the cursor. Do that for each piece of unwanted material. This may seem to be a bit of a nuisance, but, if you think about it, you will realize that the ICON is making sure that you do not throw away anything that you really still want.

Now the remaining material is work you wish to retain. Move the cursor up to the top left corner, to the clip_board icon, and press **(ACTION)**. The clip_board will be saved. Now you can exit to the editor proper.

Changing Tracking Speeds

Before I leave the main functions, let me answer what must be a burning question: Why are there two sets of crossed arrows at the top right corner?

Select the leftmost of the arrows, and then press **(ACTION)**. Now roll the trackball under your fingers. The material will move quite rapidly in whichever direction you wish it to

go. Now release **(ACTION)**, move to the right set of arrows, and do the same thing again. The material will move quite slowly for the same amount of trackball movement.

Programming the Function Keys

Even with the convenience of two tracking speeds, the need to move the cursor all over the screen to access the various icons may become annoying at times. It can be a bit of a nuisance if you wish to work fairly rapidly, ideas burning in your head, and yet you have to roll the cursor from the top down to the bottom and then to the center and then to the bottom and back and forth and so on and so forth!

Could there be a short cut, somehow? Yes, there could — and there is. Those function keys along the top can be set to perform any of the functions that the icons perform. Simply bring the cursor to the appropriate icon, and then press both **(ACTION)** and one of the functions keys at the same time.

Let us say you wish to use function key 1 (F1) to scroll rapidly. Move the cursor to the leftmost scrolling icon. Leave it there while you press both **(ACTION)** and F1. Now you no longer need move to the scrolling icon. Just press F1 and move the trackball. It works!

You can program any of the function keys in this way. May I suggest, however, that you use just one or two to begin with, to get used to the idea (and so you do not forget which is which!), and then slowly work your way up until the whole row of function keys is set. Remember that you must set them each time you enter the text editor. When you leave it, the function keys "lose their memory".

Printing Your Text

Now we come to the proof of the pudding: the printing of your text.

First, the text must be saved. Move the cursor to the notebook in the top left corner, and press **(ACTION)**. Wait while the ICON saves the material, the time it takes to do this depending on the length of the material. Then move the cursor to the door next to the pencil. After a short while, you will exit the editor and return to the shell prompt %.

At this point, you can type the letters **ls** to see that your new file is listed in your directory. You will also see a file called clip_board if you saved it as I suggested earlier. The fact that the clip_board is listed as a file is very useful, for you can access it directly without having to enter the text editor and then move to the clip_board. This is how to do it.

Merely type the letter **p**, then a space, and then the word **clip_board**. The contents of the clip_board will appear on the screen. If there is a lot of material, you will have to put your finger on the **(PAUSE)** key down in the left corner of the keyboard. This will allow you to read the material.

Any file can be read in this way. Once more, the command is this:

p (filename)

You have printed your file directly to the screen. You can read it, but you cannot edit it. If you want to edit it, you must enter the text editor.

The command to print out a hard copy (on the printer) is similar:

print (filename)

The activity light (the rectangle in the top right corner) will flash, and then the printer will begin to chatter away and print your text.

You can print both your text and your clip_board, if you wish to keep printed copies at hand. Do not believe those who say that the printed piece of paper is a thing of the past. There are often times when a sheet of paper near at hand allows work to be accomplished speedily.

When you save a new version of a file, the old version is erased and replaced by the new one. Computerists call this process *overwriting*. Hard copy of the old version allows you to keep a record for comparison. Alternatively, you can copy the old version into a different file using the QNX **copy (oldfile))(newfile)** command you used in Chapter 5. You can then edit either version. You can compare the two versions by using the command **diff (oldfile) (newfile)**.

If you ever wish to have an exact copy of what you see on the screen, including the various icons, simply press, all at the same time, **(CTRL)**, **(SHIFT)**, and ∗. The screen will turn into reverse mode, wiping downward. Soon the printer will begin to make an exact copy of the screen. That is how the figures in this book were produced.

All of this might seem to be a trifle complex at first, but, as with anything else, practice makes perfect. The index and the list of common commands, both at the back of the book, will guide you to the relevant section so that you can go over any points you have forgotten.

SUMMARY

The ICON system contains a superb editor that allows you to compose and manipulate text. Once you have accessed the editor with the command **edit (filename)**, no further commands of any sort are necessary.

First, type in your text on the keyboard as with a typewriter. Then, to perform any of the various manipulations, highlight the relevant material by moving the cursor over it while pressing **⟨ACTION⟩**; move the cursor to the appropriate icon, and press **⟨ACTION⟩** again.

Portions of the text may be removed, replaced, copied, underlined, and so on, and all portions so manipulated are stored in a file called ''clip_board''. New material, as well, may be added to the clip_board. The clip_board file, like all files, can be released when the material is no longer of use.

The text as a whole is stored as a file and may be retrieved for further editing.

The function keys can be set to perform any of the functions that the icons perform.

The ICON is multi-tasking: the same file can be both edited and printed at the same time.

It is not necessary to enter the editor in order to examine material created with it. The **p** command will bring either the text file or the clip_board to the screen. But it is necessary to enter the editor in order to edit material.

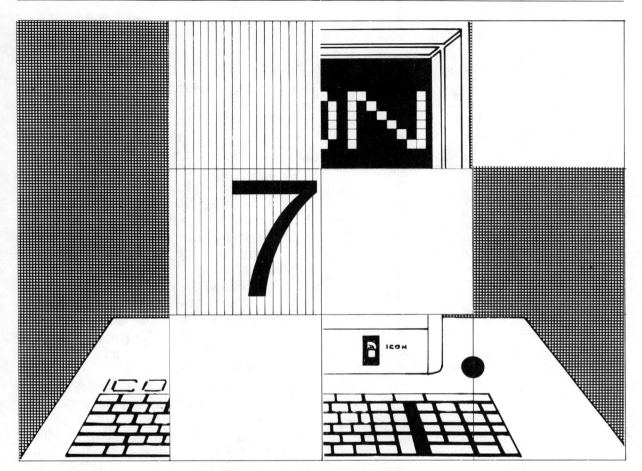

GRAPHICS IN DETAIL

USING THE ICON EDITOR

As you know, all of the ICON's programs and editors are resident in the LEXICON. In order to use one of them, you must first transfer it to your ICON work station. This process is called *downloading*. The first thing you will do in this section is download the icon editor.

To begin, you should be logged in under your own user name and password. When you see the shell prompt %, type in the following command:

ied〈ENTER〉

That's all — just the letters **ied**. They stand for "icon editor". When the editor has been downloaded to the ICON, the screen will look like Figure 7.1.

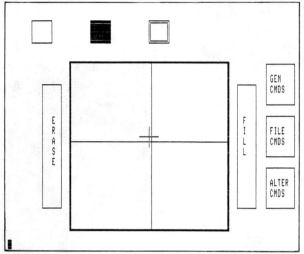

Figure 7.1   The image produced by the **ied** command.

Creating an Icon

The screen is now your drawing board, and on it you are going to create a picture in large blocks. Just as with the text editor, you will be using the trackball.

Move the trackball; remember to roll it lightly under your fingertips, keeping the thumb of the right hand ready on the ACTION key, or a finger of the left hand on the other ACTION key. You will see the cross hairs move over the screen. Move the cross hairs to the box on the right marked **GEN CMDS**, which stands for "general commands". Press 〈**ACTION**〉, and you will see four selections on the menu. Move the highlighting in the

window until it falls on **set active point**, and then release the 〈**ACTION**〉 key. Now move the cross hairs to the rectangle in the center of the screen, and press 〈**ACTION**〉 once more. Immediately the crossed lines on the screen will move to intersect where you have placed the cross hairs. Move the trackball around, keeping your thumb or finger on the 〈**ACTION**〉 key. The crossed lines will follow. Release 〈**ACTION**〉, and the crossed lines will stay where you have placed them.

Now move the trackball to bring the cross hairs to the long, vertical rectangle on the right marked **FILL**. Press 〈**ACTION**〉 and then release, and bring the cross hairs to the large central rectangle. Anywhere will do. Now press 〈**ACTION**〉 once more, and you will see a small filled rectangle appear on the screen. Move the trackball while keeping your thumb or finger on the 〈**ACTION**〉 key. The drawing will take shape as you move the trackball. Draw some kind of shape. Don't worry if you make a mistake or do something weird, producing some strange design. Just practice for a while.

If you have produced a total mess, release the 〈**ACTION**〉 key and move the trackball to bring the cross hairs to the **GEN CMDS** box once more, this time selecting the **clear screen** function. Move the trackball down to highlight the words, and then release 〈**ACTION**〉. The central area will clear, removing your drawing. Now you can start over and produce something else. You might wish to practice these moves quite a few times, trying to draw something reasonable. Figure 7.2 shows a treble clef sign I produced for a program about music.

If you wish to modify your drawing — and I am certain you will want to — move the trackball over to the rectangle marked **ERASE**.

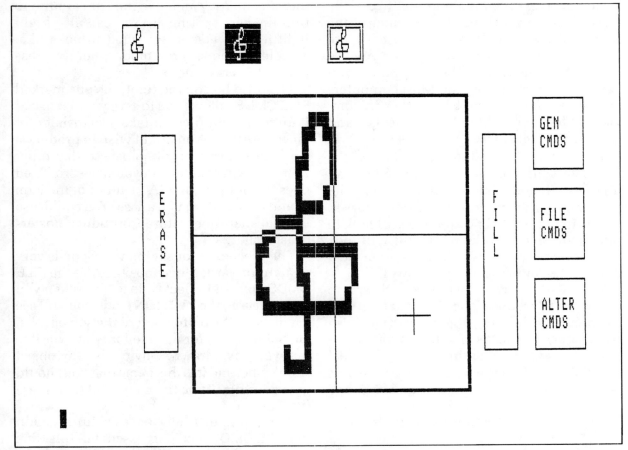

Figure 7.2   A drawing produced with the icon editor. The three small images at the top show what the icon will look like.

Press **(ACTION)** to select that function, and release. Now move the trackball to bring the cross hairs over the small block you wish to remove, and then press **(ACTION)** once more. The offending block will disappear. You can keep the **(ACTION)** key down, and wipe over a number of blocks all at once.

At this point, if you have had any experience with computers, you may well be asking what all the fuss is about the ICON's hi-res graphics. The large blocks are far removed from high-resolution, fine-scale images!

The answer is simple. The ICON is indeed capable of very high resolution graphics. The editor you are using is nothing more than a tool to draw fine-scale pictures. It is rather like a magnifying glass, enlarging the image so that you can work with it more easily.

If you look at the top of the screen, you will see three small images forming as you draw, each one an exact copy, in miniature, of the object you are graphing in the center of the screen. These miniatures, called slaves, are the exact size that they will be when you use them, the same size as the other icons you have used in the text editor. Most computers have image editors available either in commercial form or written by enthusiasts and printed in magazines.

The small images show exactly what the final icon will look like, not only in normal, unaccessed mode, but also in reverse mode, as it appears when accessed by the cursor. It is as important to know how it will look in this mode as it is to know how it will look in the other, for the icon must be quite clear in order to perform its function well.

You see, the purpose of the icon editor is to allow you to produce icons for your own special programs, inserting them where you wish for access by the users of your programs. Using icons saves a lot of time and a great deal of script. A picture is worth a thousand words — in this case, a thousand words of typing.

Storing and Retrieving Your Icon

Now make a very simple drawing. Use only the FILL and ERASE functions and, if necessary, the clear screen command from the GEN CMDS box. When you are finished, look at your drawing carefully, and see whether it needs to be moved up or down, left or right, in the drawing area. Examine the small versions at the top of the screen to judge these factors.

Move the trackball to ALTER CMDS. It is the lowest rectangle on the right. Press (ACTION).

Highlight one of the menu items and press (ACTION) again, watching what happens on the screen. You can move the icon around to find the best spot for it. You can also highlight it in reverse to see what it looks like. To release the reverse mode, merely press (ACTION) once more.

The third box on the right, the one marked FILE CMDS, allows you to save your icon, call it up from your files, or take a snapshot of it on your printer. You might wish to produce a small prompt sheet, on paper, so that other users know what the icon you have produced does to your program. A printout of the icon would be useful in such a case. You could also use the snapshot feature to produce posters or labels!

The procedure for saving your icon is very straightforward. Move the cursor to the FILE CMDS box, and select write to file. When you have released the (ACTION) key, you will see a request at the bottom left of the screen. You are being asked for a name for whatever it is that you have drawn. Obviously, any object has a name, and it is this name that you should give your file. Type the name and then press (ENTER) as usual.

Retrieving the file is just as simple. Again the FILE CMDS box is accessed, but this time the command read in file is selected. Give the name of a stored file, and in a flash the design will appear on the screen. Very simple!

USING THE GRAPHICS EDITOR

Maybe you do not want to produce icons. Maybe you would rather produce more detailed graphics, perhaps for inclusion in a program. The ICON computer has facilities to allow you to do this.

If you have not already done so, exit from ied, and then, when the shell prompt % is

returned to you on the screen, type this:
  fged test
You can use some other file name if you wish. The letters "ged" stand for "graphics editor". The "f" indicates that this is the sixth improvement of the editor. See the /util directory for an update if necessary.

  When the editor has been downloaded, you will see a screen of written instructions.

Ignore them for the moment by pressing **⟨ENTER⟩**, whereupon the screen will look like Figure 7.3. The editor is now in a state of readiness to draw lines, and you can do that directly by moving the cursor to some point in the large rectangle, pressing **⟨ACTION⟩**, and keeping it down while you move the cursor to some new point within the rectangle.

Figure 7.3 The image produced by the **fged** command.

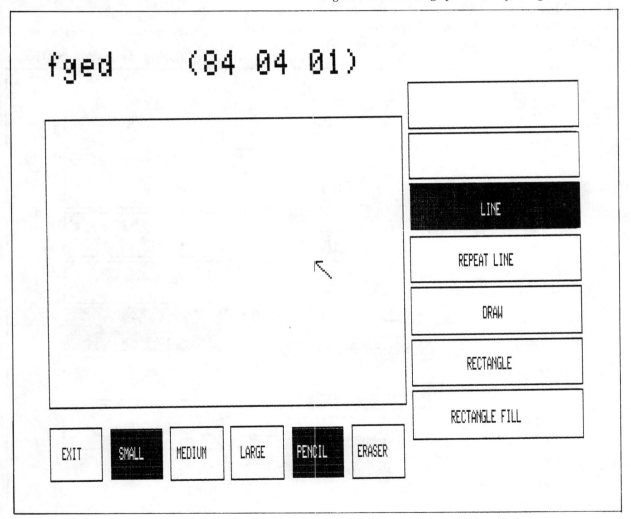

As you move the cursor, the line you are drawing will stretch out like a rubber band. In fact, this is called the "rubber band effect". When you have reached the other end of the line (when to end it is up to you, of course), release the **(ACTION)** key . . . and there is your line. Draw a few more lines to become accustomed to the effect.

Now move the trackball to bring the cursor to REPEAT LINE. Press **(ACTION)** to select this feature, and then move the cursor back to the rectangular drawing area.

Draw a line as you did before, moving the trackball to the end of your line. Release **(ACTION)**, and then move the trackball to some new point while you press **(ACTION)** again. The new line you are drawing will start at the end of the first one. This feature is very useful, allowing you to produce a series of connected lines. To quit the effect, move the cursor out of the drawing area.

By this time, you probably have something that looks like Figure 7.4(a).

Figure 7.4   Some effects you can create using the graphics editor.
(a) A printout of the graphic described in this book.

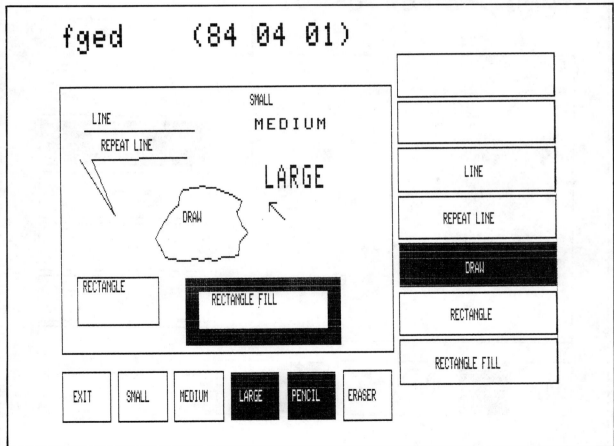

Courtesy CEMCORP/Michael Lant

(b) A photo of a different graphic on the screen.

That is all very well . . . but how to erase it?

You have probably spotted the **ERASER** command in the commands boxes. You could move directly to that command, select it, and then try to erase each line. You would find that this is not very convenient. There is a quicker way.

Bring the cursor down to **RECTANGLE FILL**, and then select it. Move the cursor to **ERASER** and select that feature. Now move the cursor and produce a rectangle that encloses everything you have drawn. Then release the **(ACTION)** key. The mess — or masterpiece — is gone.

Now select **DRAW** once more, and you can draw any shape you wish — even sign your name.

The rule with the graphics editor is exactly the same as with the other editors: First select the function by pressing **(ACTION)**, and then perform the action.

In continuous-line mode, you can break the line merely by lifting the **(ACTION)** key, moving the cursor to a new point, and then pressing **(ACTION)** for the new continuous line.

By astute use of straight and continuous lines, filled and open rectangles, you can produce all sorts of images. A filled rectangle can be the basis for a house, open rectangles the windows, and free continuous lines the trees, shrubs, and paths. Figure 7.5 is an example. Figure 1.1 (in the first chapter) was produced using this editor.

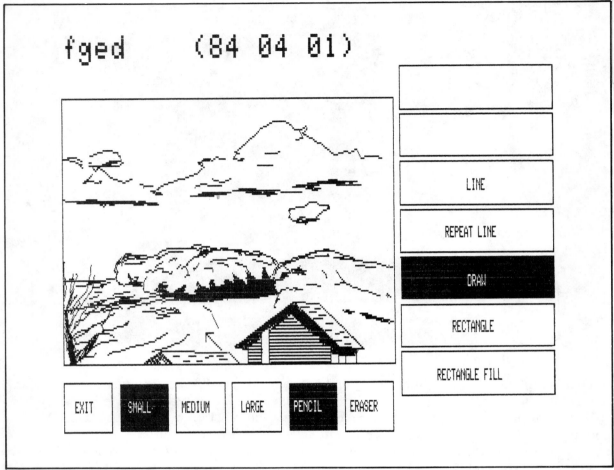

Figure 7.5   A picture drawn with the graphics editor.

When you have a masterpiece on the screen, you will want to give it a name. First make sure that you are in draw mode; then bring the cursor to the point where you would like to begin printing, and just type the words. Put the CAP LOCK key down, and put the words in upper case.

What if you have a diagram and wish to make labels that follow the contour of the lines? That effect, called *staggered print*, is easy to create. Just move the cursor for each letter before typing it. You can make the letters wave all over the screen, even overlap each other, although to make the result legible takes quite a bit of practice. The words SMALL, MEDIUM, and LARGE at the bottom of the screen refer to the sizes of letters you may type on the screen. Using the trackball, select the size you want, and then move the pointer to the spot in your drawing where you wish the words to start printing. Then type away! Figure 7.6 is an example of what you can do.

Figure 7.6 The staggered-print feature can be used to label diagrams.

There! Now all you have to do is save it! This is a very simple operation performed by moving the cursor to EXIT.

The shell prompt % will be returned to you. Now you can type the letters **ls** to see that the test file is in that directory.

To see a full-screen version of your drawing, without the commands boxes, just type this:

cat test

There you are! There is your drawing. Figure 7.7 is a full-screen version of the drawing in Figure 7.5. (You will find more examples of full-screen drawings in Appendix B, at the back of this book.)

Figure 7.7 A full-screen version of the drawing in Figure 7.5.

Images can be drawn in reverse, as with scraper board ink drawings (in which the surface is first covered with a wash of ink and the drawing produced by scraping, with a variety of implements, the dark away to reveal the light surface). First fill the drawing area with a filled rectangle. Select **ERASER** and **DRAW**. The amber ''surface'' will be ''scraped'' to reveal the dark ''surface''.

If you are buzzing with ideas of things to draw, go ahead and do that. The rest can wait while you become thoroughly familiar with the trackball and the commands.

For each drawing you make, provide a suitably descriptive file name. Planning what you are going to draw before you begin, rather than just doodling, will allow you to do some useful work with the graphic a little later on.

Having decided that you are going to draw a house, type that as the file name before you press **⟨ENTER⟩** to get to that actual graphics work area.

You will be asked which line number you wish to start at. You can use any line number you wish, but it is better to start at a reasonably high one so that you can merge the drawing with a normally produced BASIC program. If you know how to program in BASIC, try the activity described in the next section.

ADDING GRAPHICS TO
A BASIC PROGRAM

Enter the line number. Produce your drawing, being as careful as you can. Then exit by typing ∧c.

Call up Watcom BASIC and write a short introductory program describing what the user is about to see.

End your program with a line number lower than the one you selected for your graphic; if your graphic begins at line number 2000, then make your BASIC program end with line number 1999, and place the following command there:

1999 print chr$(12)

This will clear the screen of any text before displaying your graphic.

Now, *without a line number*, type the following command:

merge test.bas

The ICON will respond with a total number of lines for your program. Save it as you normally would, and then run it.

To see a listing of the entire program on the screen, including the syscalls (see Chapter 10 for further details on these), merely type **list** or just the letter **l**, followed by **⟨ENTER⟩**. You will see just one screenful of your program. To see further lines, just press **⟨ENTER⟩**.

USING THE FONT EDITOR

There is a third image editor available that allows the production of special kinds of type, or fonts, such as Medieval, Hebrew, Russian, and Devenagri. It is reached by this command:

font_ed or **fed**

It works in the same way as ied, the icon editor, except that a font must be saved and written to a file in order to be reached when required. Note: This editor is so new at the time of writing that some of the features are not yet implemented, and full documentation is not yet available. By the time this book is published, that situation will have been remedied.

If you choose to explore this editor, remember to leave blank squares on two sides of your letter so that there will be a space between them when printed to the screen. This pre- caution might well prove to be unnecessary, but it cannot hurt.

SUMMARY

Three editors allow users to produce graphic images.

The icon editor allows you to create icons to substitute for commands in your own programs. Enter the editor with the command **ied**. As you create and refine a large image, smaller replicas of it indicate what its final appearance will be. You can save, call up, and print your icons.

The graphics editor allows you to produce complex and detailed graphics. Enter with the command **ged (filename)**. The chapter explained how to insert graphics in a BASIC program.

The third image editor produces special type fonts. Full documentation is not yet available.

THE DEEPER MYSTERIES OF QNX

USING QNX AS A
PROGRAMMING LANGUAGE

In Chapter 5, a comment was made to the effect that QNX, although an operating system, works like a programming language. It contains commands that can be strung together in a file, called a *command file*, and used as a program. An example is in order here, but I am going to formulate the process in the language BASIC first so that a comparison can be made. I must, of course, assume that you have some knowledge of BASIC.

The tasks our program is going to perform are to allow input of a number of names according to the user's choice, to sort them into alphabetical order, and then to print the result on the screen.

If you wish, you may enter the BASIC program on the ICON. To do so, first type this:

basic

You may then enter the program. For further comments on entering BASIC programs, refer to Chapter 10.

```
100 dim a$(20)
110 print "How many names?"
120 input n
130 for k = 1 to n
140 input a$(k)
150 next k
160 print "Now sorting. Please wait"
170 for k = 1 to n-1
180 if a$(k+1) ) = a$(k) then 230
190 b$ = a$(k+1)
200 a$(k+1) = a$(k)
210 a$(k) = b$
220 goto 170
230 next k
240 for i = 1 to n
250 print a$(i)
260 next i
270 end
```

I should, perhaps, apologize for producing a program that includes one of those horrid "goto" statements. I have produced a program in the form most likely to be familiar to people who have not had the opportunity to work with structured BASIC. The program performs what is known as a *bubble sort*. Each letter of the alphabet is pushed to the next topmost position, in much the same way as bubbles push themselves to the top of a liquid. It is likely that students will have typed a pro-

gram of this sort into other, smaller machines and noted how slowly the sorting occurs with a large number of names. The slowness is due partly to the language BASIC, partly to the machine, and partly to the bubble-sort algorithm.

When the program has been typed in very carefully and checked for accuracy, save it by typing this command:

save namesort.bas

Then run the program by typing this command:

run

The limit to the number of names is set at 20. You can change this by altering the number in parentheses in line 100, but you should start with a small number of names.

You can enhance the program just a little by adding the following line:

235 print chr$(12)

This will clear the screen for you before the sorted list appears.

Good! Now you are going to do the same thing using QNX commands.

Exit from BASIC by typing this word:

bye

The % sign will appear. Now type this word:

clearscreen

The ICON screen will clear.

Now type this command:

edit namesort.qnx

The ICON editor will appear, complete with icons.

Move the cursor to the top left corner, and enter the following exactly as you see it:

```
clearscreen
type     This is an example of using QNX
         as a "programming language"
wait_for_char
clearscreen
```

type	Thankyou
type	Enter a list of names
type	Press ⟨ENTER⟩ after each name
type	Press ⟨CTRL⟩ d to finish your entry
copy ⟩ names	
clearscreen	
sort names	
type	Thankyou

Save the program, and exit from the editor. (If you do not recall how to do these things, refer to Chapter 6.)

When you have left the editor, the % sign will appear once more. Change the attributes so that the program may be executed, by typing this command:

chattr namesort.qnx a = + e

Now you can use the program. Merely type this:

namesort.qnx

Now follow the instructions you see on the screen. Do not forget to type ∧d when you have finished entering names.

The explanation of the program or command file is as follows:

clearscreen	clears the screen
type	the equivalent of BASIC **print**
wait_for_char	the equivalent of BASIC **get** or **INKEY$**
copy	copies from the keyboard input
⟩	sends the keyboard input to a file called "names"
sort	sorts the contents of "names" and prints the result on the screen

It would be grossly unfair to compare the speeds with which the QNX and BASIC sort long lists, because the bubble sort, even on the ICON, can be extremely slow. The important thing to notice is the greater efficiency of operating-system commands.

If you type the command

ls

(which stands for "list sorted"), you will see that you have not just one but two new files: **namesort.bas** and **names**. The first one was created by you when you typed in the program and saved it from the editor. The second was created when you ran the program or command file. If you issue the command

p names

you will see the names *in the order in which you typed them on the keyboard*. If you execute the file again (the proper expression for "run a program") with different names, then once more type the command

p names

you will find that the old contents have disappeared and have been replaced by the new names. If you wish to keep the old set of names, you must change (edit) the namesort.qnx file so that the new file generated is different from the old one, perhaps by calling the new one "names2".

Alternatively, you can include a set of commands that will allow a new list to be appended to the old. Further enhancement could allow the sorted list to be piped to a new file, thus providing you with the original data and the sorted version.

SPECIAL PRINTING COMMANDS

You have already dealt with the command **p**. It merely prints the file on the screen. The command **print** sends the file to the printer. However, caution must be exercised here, for the command **print** sends the file to only one kind of printer — namely, one of the parallel variety. As you know, the other kind of printer supported by the ICON system is known as "serial". Some printers support both means of accepting data from the computer, but you must be sure that the cable connection is plugged into the correct socket.

If the printer connected to the LEXICON is serial, then you must issue a different command:

sprint

Likewise, if you wish to list a file on the printer — a BASIC program, say — you must issue the command **slist** for serial printers or **list** for parallel printers.

Letters can be added to the various types of print and list commands to achieve particular effects. These letters are known as *options*.

When a file is printed, there are certain "default" settings; that is, the printed version will have a number of features unless you specify otherwise.

The normal printed output will have the date, time, file name, and page number at the top of each page. Together these items make up the *header*. For some documents, it is useful not to have a header. You arrange for this by adding one of the option letters to the command **print**, in the same way that you add option letters to the **chattr** command. The option to add is **-h**, so the whole command will be this:

print -h (filename)

If your file is printed on several pages, the pages will automatically be numbered successively. Let us say, however, that you are writing a book. Each chapter is contained in a separate file. For example, this book has files named icon1.txt, icon2.txt, icon3.txt, and so on. To print out each file would mean that, unless other arrangements were made, the first page of each chapter would be numbered 1. That, quite clearly, would not be very good. There is an option that prevents the page numbering from being reset to 1. It is **-r**, so that the print command will now appear as follows:

print -h -r (filename)

To turn the options back on again, the letter is preceded by a plus (**+**) sign, thus:

print +h +r (filename)

It could be that the document you wish to produce is a multipage letter. It is not normal to paginate letters, and so, to suppress the page numbers (and the headers at the same time, incidentally), you must add the option **-p**, thus:

print -p

Obviously, to turn the pagination back on, you give the option a plus sign, thus:

print +p

Some printers support special printing modes, such as emphasized print or double print. The commands in this book all appear in boldface type, but when I print the copy on my printer, prior to sending it to the publisher, I use an option that causes the commands to appear in double-print mode: each letter is overstruck so that it appears denser. The option letter for this is **+d**. Emphasized mode causes the printer to print each dot both in the regular position and just a fraction to the right of that. The print is thus darker because some of the tiny gaps between the round dots are filled with ink. The option letter for this is **+ e**. Double-print and emphasized modes together produce a good image.

In all the above cases, the options appear *before* the file name, thus:

print -h -r +d icon2.txt

The **txt** after the period in the file name is a note to myself to indicate that the file contains text and is not a BASIC or Pascal program.

If you are using a serial printer, then each of the commands will be in the format **sprint (options) (filename)**.

If you are writing a term paper or an article for a magazine, it is useful to be able to create margins in which the instructor's or publisher's notes may be penciled. It is also usually a good plan to leave double spaces between lines; in fact, magazine and book publishers insist on it, so that words may be added between the lines.

Spacing between lines is set by the option **s** followed by a number. The number refers to the number of lines per inch and is usually set to 6. For double spacing, therefore, the number 12 will follow the **s**. The normal number of characters per line is 80. The screen of your ICON will display this unless you set the tabs and margins on the editor for other values. The option letter for characters-per-line is **w**. I set mine at 66, which gives about an inch on each side of the page. The two options are followed by an equals sign (=) and then the number, thus:

print s = 8 w = 66

If you are using the ICON in school to produce examples of your computer-science activities, then it might be useful for the instructor to know your user number — the number assigned to you by the site administrator when the password file was edited. To cause your user number to appear automatically on each page, use the **+u** option.

Note that all of these options are quite independent of any tab settings or spacings you might use with the ICON editor. They are not actually QNX commands but have been created especially for use on the ICON. You can leave your ICON editor text in single-spacing mode but cause the output to be in double-spaced mode. You can ignore the tabs and margins on the editor and cause one copy to be 66 characters wide and another 80.

In large organizations, where there are a lot of people using the printing facilities, the files are "queued"; that is, instead of all the several bits and pieces of each person's file being mixed up, the fileserver keeps a note of who is first, second, third, and so on in line. Quite often, the resultant printouts are not picked up until some time after the print instruction has been issued.

How on earth can you sort out what belongs to you?

It is the general practice for each piece of work to bear a banner printed in large letters (showing date, time, and file name) or for the printout to be preceded by a separate, identifying sheet of paper. This makes it very easy to spot the work without having to paw through a vast pile of paper. To give your work a banner, simply add the option **+ b**, thus:

print +b (filename)

You may wish to cause the printout to be offset from the left margin by a certain amount, in which case you must provide a setting for the option **o**, as follows:

print o = 10

A full statement of offset, width, and spacing will therefore look like this:

print s = 12 w = 66 o = 10

This will actually leave a wider margin on the left than on the right, as a test will verify.

Either create a short piece of text or use one you have already typed, and experiment with the options in various combinations.

ACCESSING FILES ON THE DISKETTE

You will already have made extensive use of the **ls** command and probably of the **files** and **files +v** commands too. These commands will tell you what can be found on the hard disk. What if you wish to know what is on a diskette, or drive 2?

Quite simple! Type this command:

ls 2:/

or this:

files 2:/

or this:

files +v 2:/

The **+v** in the last example is an option that, as explained in Chapter 2, shows all the details of the files. (By the way, never leave your floppy disk in the LEXICON, and never power down the LEXICON with a diskette in the diskette drive.)

USING THE LOCATE UTILITY

There is a utility in QNX called "locate". When people write or speak, they often overuse certain words. For a long time, I was in the habit of using the word "indulge" far too often. I did not notice the overuse, but other people did!

It can be a great nuisance to have to go through a manuscript word by word, line by line, page by page, searching for just one word and keeping a count of how many times it has been used. Likewise with misspelled words or words that are spelled differently in different parts of the world. For example, one of the icons you see in the ICON editor shows a pair of glasses. In the first version of my manuscript, I called them "spectacles", but later I decided to use the word "glasses", as that is the word generally used in the ICON documentation. First of all, I wanted to find out how many times the word "spectacles" occurred in the chapter. The command I issued was this:

locate spectacles iconed

The order of the command is thus the following:

command item-to-be-searched-for file

In seconds I was told the answer! I was given each line number of the text in which the word occurred and also the entire sentence. It appeared that the frequency was sufficient for me to use the ICON editor to perform the changes.

The command issued was this:

edit iconed

This command placed my whole text in the work-station work space. I highlighted the whole area to be searched by placing the cursor at the beginning of the passage and wiping down with the fast scroll.

Next, I placed the cursor over the search-and-replace icon next to the pencil pot. I typed in the word **spectacles**, and a window opened with the word appearing as I typed. Then I tapped the **⟨ACTION⟩** key. A small arrow appeared next to the word, and I was able to type in the word **glasses**. I tapped the **⟨ACTION⟩** key once more, and each instance of the word "spectacles" was replaced with the word "glasses".

Of course, when you are sure you want to replace a word, regardless of the number of times it appears, then there is no real need to use the **locate** command.

COMPARING FILES

A book, article, or paper is rarely written straight through without revisions. Sometimes two or more versions exist of either the whole thing or certain sections. Again, to search through each version noting differences can be irksome. The QNX operating system has a utility that allows you to find out the difference between two versions very quickly.

To test this utility, prepare two files as follows.

Enter the ICON editor by typing this command:

edit version1

Then type these words:

This is version one.

Save the text and then exit the editor.

Reenter the editor by typing this command:

edit version2

Now select the pencil icon, press **(ACTION)**, and then select the edit new file option from the menu. Then type the file name **version2**, pressing **(ACTION)** when you have finished.

Now type these words:

This is version two.

Save, exit the editor once more, and then type this command:

diff version1 version2

Immediately the two lines will appear on the screen for comparison.

Long documents, in which many lines differ, can provide one of two results. Either each pair of differing lines will be presented on the screen or, if there are a great number of differences, the computer will hiccup and tell you that there are too many differences to cope with.

OTHER USEFUL COMMANDS

If you wish to know the size of a file, merely type the command **size** followed by the file name. The result will be shown in this form:

no of chars no of lines: filename

There will be times when you wish to have material displayed on the screen in larger character size than normal. The standard, or default, resolution for the ICON is 80 characters per screen line. You can change this to 40 characters simply by typing this command:

lo_res

Note the underscore between the **lo** and the **res**.

To revert to the normal mode, simply issue this command:

hi_res

Try typing something in each mode to observe the difference.

Now enter the ICON editor with this command:

edit

Select the pencil icon and the edit new file option. Type the command

sample_res

and press **(ACTION)**. Now type the following exactly as you see it:

clearscreen	
lo_res	
type	This is the 40-column screen output
hi_res	
type	This is the 80-column screen output

Remember to provide the execute attribute by typing this command:

chattr sample a = + e

Then call up the file by typing the file name.

If you call up the Logo language, you can see the 40-column mode used as the standard for small children. Figure 8.1 shows the size of the letters as they appear in 40-column mode.

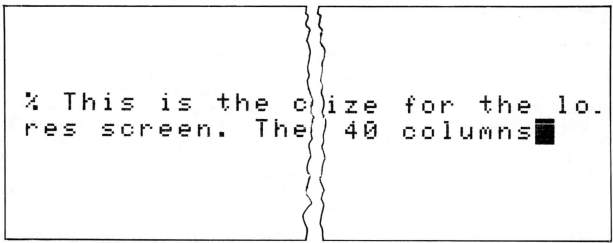

Figure 8.1   Type size produced by the **lo_res** command.

Finally, a small clutch of simple commands.

If you should happen to enter an incorrect line after a shell prompt %, there is a small chance that the ICON will get into a mess. Always check lines carefully before pressing the **(ENTER)** key. An incorrect line can be deleted in one stroke by pressing **(CTRL)** and the letter **x** (∧**x**). Try it and see!

(CTRL) **d** (∧**d**) is not only the means of logging out but also the means of exiting from keyboard input mode after a **cat** or **copy** command.

A screen can be cleared by pressing **(CTRL)** and the letter **l** (∧**l**).

If the cursor should disappear from the screen, you can bring it back by pressing **(CTRL)** and the hyphen (∧**-**).

Some long tasks may tie up your terminal while they are performed. They can be sent to the background so that other commands can be issued and executed. The format is this:

(command) &

For example:

sort file1)masterfile &

A task identity number (task ID) will appear on the screen. Take note of it, just in case you wish to stop, or "kill", the background task. A task may be "killed" with this command:

kill (taskID) (e.g., **kill 7407**)

There are, of course, many more features to QNX, and it is likely that more will be added.

Explore the system by generating your own command files such as the namesort and sample files discussed in this chapter.

84

SUMMARY

The QNX operating system is addressed by means of commands. These commands can be typed directly on the keyboard, for individual treatment by the ICON, or can be grouped in a cluster, created by using the text editor, and treated as a QNX program, or command file. A command file can be created to perform any series of acts that the user wishes. The limits are those of the imagination and knowledge of the user.

The printing commands **list** and **print** must be replaced by **slist** and **sprint** for serial printers.

Unless you specify otherwise, the printed pages will have certain headings and spacing and be numbered in a particular way. To change those features, add option letters to the print command *before* the file name.

Option 2 gives access to material on the diskette. Use the command **ls 2:/** or **files 2:/** or **files +v 2:/** to see the files on the floppy disk.

Use the locate utility to find all instances of a particular word.

Other QNX commands allow you to compare two versions of a text, find out the size of a file, see a larger type size on the screen, and more.

INPUT AND OUTPUT USING BASIC

You have played, to a small extent, with sending output from a file to the printer. Each time you issue the command **print**, the contents of your file, so far generated via the text editor, are sent to a buffer in the fileserver, and then sent to the printer. Usually, as you well know, the output from a file is sent to the screen.

In order to help you understand what is happening, I will discuss input/output redirection now.

Even as recently as 20 years ago, the normal way to "converse" with computers was to give instructions via a keyboard and to get the results from a teletype printer. The BASIC command **PRINT** dates from those days when output was printed on paper.

Nowadays, the normal method is to output to the screen — either a TV screen or a monitor. To get the output to go to some other device, you have to issue a specific instruction.

Where the output goes depends, of course,

on the command issued. A **save** command will not send a file to the screen, because the screen is not a permanent storage device and cannot save anything. Nor will that command send output to the printer, because it, too, is unable to save anything. Likewise, a request to read a file will never go to the printer.

When the instruction **save** is issued, the information is stored on the hard disk in the fileserver. When you call up a file, the output normally goes to the screen, as I have said.

If you write a program in BASIC, again the output will be on the screen, unless you give other instructions.

The printer can be attached either to the fileserver or, if you have the proper interface, to the student station. There is a difference in behavior, however, according to where it is attached. It will print, of course, but what it will print will differ.

When attached to the fileserver, the printer will obey the instructions of every ICON in the system, queuing the work from each station in order. When attached to just one ICON, the printer will obey only the instructions sent from that station. In fact, as far as the printer is concerned, the other stations will not exist, unless you give special commands that are beyond the scope of this chapter.

PRINTING HARD COPY OF YOUR PROGRAM

Let us say you wish the computer to count from 1 to 10, printing each number on the printer rather than on the screen. The program listing will not appear, of course, but only the results achieved by running the program.

Call up BASIC by typing **basic** as before, and, when the word Ready appears, enter the following program:

```
10 ! printer test
20 open #2, "test", output
30 for x = 1 to 10
40 print #2,x
50 next x
60 close #2
70 stop
```

A detailed breakdown of the program follows:

Line 10 gives the title of the program. The exclamation point tells the computer that the material that follows is not to be printed or acted on in any way.

Line 20 opens a channel to a file. This file is going to be called "test", and the result of running the program will go into that file. Note that the file name is in quotes this time.

Line 30 is the first half of the loop that counts up to 10.

Line 40 prints the value of x as it moves through 1 to 10. Note that the channel number indicates that the result of the counting is to go into the file called "test".

Line 50 is the second half of the loop begun on line 30.

Line 60 closes the channel opened in line 20.

Line 70 stops the program.

Save the program by calling it some name other than "test".

Now run it.

It will seem as if nothing has happened. Certainly nothing will have appeared on the screen. However, if you leave BASIC, by typing the word **bye**, and then type the letters **ls** at the next shell prompt %, you will see your program test listed among your files in your directory.

Now, to see the result, issue this command:

print test

Soon the printer will print the numbers 1 to 10 on the page. You already know, no doubt, that you could get the numbers printed across the page instead of down it. I will leave you to play with that as you wish.

It should be quite clear to you that the file could have contained names just as well as numbers. In fact, a set of names together with a set of marks, union or society dues, attendance at meetings — anything you like — can be dealt with in just as simple a fashion.

Call up BASIC, then call up the program you have just written, by typing this command:

old test

Within seconds, the program will be loaded into the ICON memory.

List the program on the screen, and then edit the lines as follows (don't worry about the changes. You will save the new program under another name):

```
10 !names
20 open #2, "names", output
25 ?"Enter 10 names one at a time"
30 for i = 1 to 10
35 input x$
40 print #2,x$
50 next i
60 close #2
70 stop
```

You have changed the name of the file to which the output is going, and you have added a line that allows you to input a series of names. Save the program under the file name "list", or anything other than "names".

Now run the program, entering names in any order you like.

Again, nothing will seem to happen. Exit from BASIC and then type **ls**.

There you will see the new file **names** listed among the others in your directory. In order to see the output, you must type this command:

print names

The names will be printed on the page exactly as you entered them. You could also type this command:

p names

In this case, the list of names would appear on the screen instead of on paper.

INPUT AND OUTPUT FROM FILE TO FILE

Let us continue our exploration of input/output redirection.

Not only can you redirect output to different devices. You can also redirect it to different files, have some sort of work done on the contents, and then see the results either on the screen or on paper — even send the result to yet a new file for storage. Thus, you can keep the raw data and the result in two separate places, just in case someone wishes to see the raw data at any time.

You already have some raw data to work on — a list of names. First you must send the contents of your directory to a file called "temp". Do it this way:

files)temp

The) sign can be found just to the left of the question mark.

As soon as the shell prompt is returned, issue this command:

sort names

The result is a set of names sorted into alphabetical order on the screen.

You could alter the program to be a little more practical, as follows:

```
10 !marks
20 open #2, "marks", output
30 print "Enter name and mark at each
         prompt"
40 for i = 1 to 10
50 ?"Name and mark"
60 input x$
70 print #2,x$
80 next i
90 close #2
100 stop
```

The name and mark are treated as one string. The output will go to a file called "marks".

The program can be saved under a file name such as "score".

To see the result on the screen or printer, you must first exit BASIC and then issue the command to **print** or **p marks**. Then issue the command to send the output to a temporary file, and then have it sorted; then send the result to another file, and print it.

Let me make it quite clear that this is what you would do from a BASIC program. You would perform a similar activity in a Pascal program, too, of course.

As you might well expect, there is a quicker way to produce a list of students and their marks, members and their dues, customers and their purchases, items and their cost, or whatever. You can use the operating system. In fact, as must be obvious to you by now, that is exactly what you did when you issued

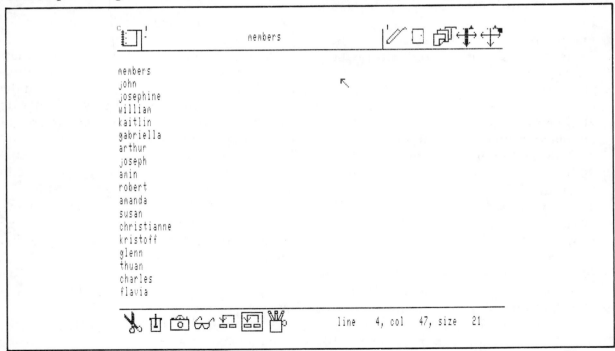

Figure 9.1   An unsorted list of names.

the **sort** and **)** commands. You are going to be quicker this time, though.

This is how to do it. First, issue this command:

edit members

Then enter your list. The screen will look something like Figure 9.1.

```
% sort members


amanda
amin
arthur
charles
christianne
flavia
gabriella
glenn
john
joseph
josephine
kaitlin
kristoff
members
robert
susan
thuan
william
%
```

Figure 9.2   The list of names from Figure 9.1, after sorting.

When you have finished, exit through the door, and then issue this command:

sort members

The result will look something like Figure 9.2.

Now, that is not exactly what you wanted, is it? The title seems to have got mixed up in there somehow. The sort utility worked on the entire contents of the file, including the title, because, as far as the computer is concerned, the title is part of the file. It is a better plan to add titles and any other material *after* you have sorted the parts you want sorted.

Now this still seems to be a bit inconvenient. Isn't there a much better way? The answer, which you surely have guessed by now, is yes.

Instead of issuing the command to enter the editor, merely direct the screen to copy from the keyboard. The command is in the form **copy)(filename)**.

So issue the command in the following way:

copy)names

The **)** symbol is obtained with SHIFT period.

The shell prompt % disappears, but the cursor moves to the next line. Now type your list of names, such as the following, pressing **⟨ENTER⟩** after each name:

john
jim
joan
jennifer
Julie
James

Now type
⟨CTRL⟩d
and then
p names
and then on the screen is the list, just as you typed it.

Now type this command:
sort names
The result is still a little bit odd:

James
Julie
jennifer
jim
joan
john

You will notice that the names beginning with upper-case letters have been sorted first, and then the alphabetization starts again with the lower-case letters. This is because of the way the ASCII code is organized. (ASCII stands for American Standard Code for Information Interchange — a standard order in which letters of the alphabet, punctuation marks, numerals, and special characters are handled by computers.) Just be sure that you start all names with upper-case letters, and be consistent in other kinds of lists so that you do not achieve bizarre results.

You can enter anything you like after the cursor. You are not limited to just one item per line. Enter a collections list as follows:

```
copy )collections
Josephine      $200
Jennifer       $123
Joan           $79
Jeremy         $140
June           $90
```

Then type ∧**d** as before, to exit the copy mode; then issue the command **sort collections**, whereupon the list will be sorted.

If you now type the letters **ls**, you will see the file **collections** among those you already have.

Now type this command:

p collections

Do not worry if you see ＼CC＼CC＼CC in front of the list. Note that the command causes the *raw data* to be shown. In order to see the sorted list, you must issue a command to sort the data, send it to a new file, and then print *that* file.

This has been a relatively quick tour of the business of redirection of input and output, but I am sure you can see that the facilities are very, very flexible, allowing use of redirection from the programming languages as well as the QNX operating system.

<table><tr><td>▦▦▦▦▦</td><td></td><td>SUMMARY</td><td></td><td>▦▦▦▦▦</td></tr></table>

When a program is created in any one of the languages available on the ICON, and saved, a file is created. Similarly, any output from such a program can be given a file name and the contents called up separately.

The ICON treats devices as if they were files stored in the computer; thus, the output from a file can be sent either to another file containing data or to a physical device (such as the screen or the printer). The process is called *redirection*.

Direct use of operating-system commands is often the fastest method of redirection. Users who are more familiar with procedures found in languages such as BASIC will find the ICON treatment of files and devices very convenient.

PROGRAMMING GRAPHICS IN BASIC

STRUCTURED BASIC

It is more than likely that you already know how to program in the language called BASIC. It is probable that you are familiar with one of the varieties of this language commonly available on the most popular machines found in schools and homes. If you have worked (or played) with computers from various manufacturers, you will already know that BASIC takes various forms. You will have heard that BASIC is not a very good language — that it provides too much flexibility and that some forms are worse in this regard than others, encouraging poor programming habits. The truth is that the English language is also very flexible, and one can find poor users of that language, too, as one can of German, Chinese, or Russian.

In an attempt to produce organized BASIC programmers, programmers who think and work logically, some people have produced what is known as *structured BASIC*. As you might expect, there is more than one variety of structured BASIC. All the varieties are designed to produce code that is clear enough to allow users of programs—users other than the original authors—to modify programs or transfer them to other computers. A side benefit of structured BASIC is that it allows school teachers to mark and assess a student's program more readily.

The brand of structured BASIC used on the ICON is Waterloo BASIC, or Watcom BASIC. It is a very powerful language, rich in vocabulary, allowing for clear and concise design of programs. There are many similarities with other dialects, of course; most of the commands and statements will be familiar, and you should have little difficulty in using the language.

I have no intention of teaching you how to use Waterloo BASIC. A full text would be necessary for that. I am, however, going to show you one or two features that will intrigue you and that I hope you will find useful.

First of all, it is important to note that *there must be a space after each command or statement*. Some forms of BASIC will allow you to write this:

FORI = 1TO20:

Waterloo BASIC will not allow you to do that.

The line must be in this form:

for i = 1 to 20:

Note the lower-case characters! You can code in upper case if you like, of course, but it is not necessary.

LOADING BASIC

BASIC is already stored on the hard disk. All you have to do is call it up and wait for it to load.

You should have logged on and given your password to place yourself in your home directory. It is a good plan to keep all your BASIC programs separate from other files, and so you will now make a directory for BASIC programs. You should have the shell prompt on the screen:

%

Type the following:

mkdir basic⟨ENTER⟩

If you now type the letters **ls**, you will see a listing of all files and directories under your home directory. One of them will be this:

+ basic

The cross in front of the name indicates that it is a directory. Before you can work in that directory, however, you must change to it, by typing this:

cd basic

The ICON will return the shell prompt % to you once more. Now you can load BASIC simply by typing this:

basic

That's all—just **basic**. Then press **⟨ENTER⟩** as usual.

USING THE KEY-PAD FOR EDITING

After a flicker or two of the activity rectangle in the top right corner, the ICON will return with a message saying that the language is loaded, and the familiar BASIC prompt Ready will appear on the screen.

You are ready to begin. Before you do so, however, I am going to give you some guidelines.

A lot of people have become accustomed to machines without numeric keys along the top of the keyboard. They have formed the habit of entering line numbers by means of the key-pad to the right. It is not a bad habit, yet the key-pad on the ICON can be very useful as an editing device. To use it that way, you must press down on the CUR LOCK key just above the HELP key. The little red light will come on. Now the numeric keys 1,2,3, and 5 become cursor-control keys for use in BASIC. Try to form the habit of using the top row of numeric keys for entering digits and the key-pad for editing. Otherwise you will find it necessary to change constantly between editing and numeric modes. This can be frustrating, particularly if you are working rapidly.

HI-RES GRAPHICS USING WATCOM BASIC

Here is a short program:

```
10 x% = syscall%(210)
30 fp% = syscall%(138,x%,.0,.0,.5,.5)
```

Type it exactly as you see it. It is the short introductory program that I wrote for the CEMCORP ICON *Training Manual* — which is why it may be familiar to you!

Now type the word **run**.

A straight line will appear starting in the bottom left-hand corner, as in Figure 10.1.

Now! Using the cursor-control keys on the key-pad (you should have the cursor lock down, and the light should be on), bring the cursor up to line 30, move it along to the third and fourth digits (**.5,.5**), and change one of them, being careful to ensure that you have a decimal value — point something-or-other — and that the values are separated by a comma. Do not let your value go higher than decimal nine (.9), however.

Try changing the third digit to .7, for example. You should still have the command run on the screen, so just press **(ENTER)** when the cursor reaches that command. Do you see what happens to your line? The start point is the same, but your finish point has changed.

Bring the cursor back up to line 30, and change the third digit to .3. Now you have three lines on the screen. They begin at the same point but end at different points.

Using smart programming techniques, it is possible to produce the same thing in a much more efficient fashion. In fact, you can easily produce something much fancier. Add the following lines:

```
20 for i = .1 to .8 step .05   (Remember the spaces!)
40 next i
```

Now bring the cursor up to line 30, move it along to the third digit, and press the key on the key-pad marked DEL, just once.

Now go back one space to the decimal point and press the letter i in place of the .3 or .5 that you have at the moment. Remember to remove the decimal point. To clean up the act a little more, add this line:

5 ? chr$(12)

Your program should now look like this:

---

5 ? chr$(12)
10 x% = syscall%(210)
20 for i = .1 to .8 step .05
30 fp% = syscall%(138,x%,.0,.0,i,.5)
40 next i

Now run your program by typing **run** or just the letter **r**.

To see the listing on the screen at the same time as the graphic, press **l** (there is no need to type the whole word **list**). The program listing will "eat" part of your graphic, but don't worry.

Now bring the cursor up to line 20 and move it along to the value by which the increment is stepped — the .05 after the word step.

Change the value to .02, so that your line now reads this way:

20 for i = .1 to .8 step .02

Now run the program once more (line 5 clears the screen for you so that it will not get cluttered).

You must admit that the result is fairly neat! Now you will do something even more clever. You are going to nest another for-next loop inside the one you already have and then see

Figure 10.1   A line drawn using syscall 138.

Figure 10.2   A program using nested for-next loops to create multiple lines.

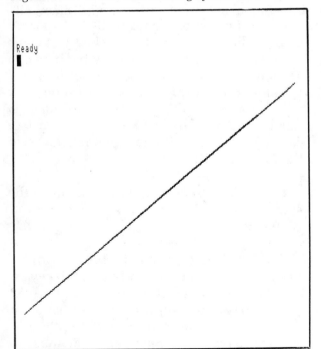

```
l
pattern3 84/08/02 19:53:46

   5 print chr$(12)
  10 x%=syscall%(210)
  20 for i = .1 to .9 step .07
  22 for z=.8 to .1 step -.09
  30 fp%=syscall%(138,x%,.0,z,i,.8)
  38 next z
  40 next i
Ready
```

the effect. Copy the new lines and alter the old ones according to the listing in Figure 10.2. When you have made sure your copy is exact, run the program.

The ICON works pretty fast, don't you think?

Perhaps you would like to save this program for future reference, as a tool from which to build other programs. Type the word **save**, followed by a space and then a file name — perhaps something like **pattern1** (no space between **pattern** and **1**!). Your command will be as follows:

save pattern1 ⟨ENTER⟩

Note that there are no quotation marks surrounding the file name!

The ICON will quickly come back with a message telling you how many lines the program consists of, and the prompt Ready.

Now go back to your original two-line program. Just type in the program lines 20, 22, 38, and 40, pressing ⟨ENTER⟩ after each one. Now press ∧l (⟨CTRL⟩ letter l) to clear the screen and then the letter l once more by itself, followed by ⟨ENTER⟩.

You will see all the lines that you have used so far, but only two of them will have any contents. Do not worry about it! The empty lines really are empty.

Rectangles

Move the cursor up to line 30 and then along to the number 138. Change it, by simply typing over the numbers, to 146. Change the values back to .0,.0,.5,.5 as before. Now run your program!
Aha! Now you can generate rectangles.

Notice that the bottom left corner of the rectangle is still at the bottom left corner of the screen and that the top right corner of the rectangle is in the center of the screen.

What happens if you change one of the .5s? What happens if you alter one of the .0s? Try a variety of values, but do not lose track of what you are doing. Save the variations you produce by giving each one a new file name — something like pattern2, pattern3, and so on.

Solid Rectangles

When you have played with that for a little while, change the 146 in line 30 to 147, and then run.

Now you have filled rectangles!

Use the programs listed above, including the nested for-next loops, and see what you can come up with. The primary rules are these: keep it all very simple, save your efforts, and do not get lost! Observe very carefully what happens to each version.

Take a look at figures 10.3 and 10.4. The last four decimal numbers in lines 30 to 32 are the important ones. These are the digits that place your figure on the screen. The first number is the start-point value for the x axis; the second digit is the start point for the y axis. The third is the finish point for the x axis *relative to the start point*. Explore this awhile by changing the values found in Figure 10.4. See what you can discover. To give yourself some ideas, put in some (or all, if you wish) of the following lines one at a time, noting the effect of each one. Do not forget to put **fp% = syscall%** in front of each one.

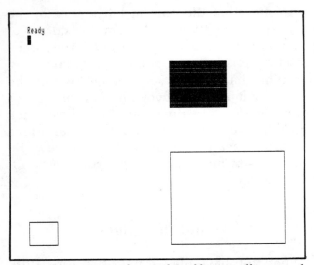

Figure 10.3   Rectangles produced by syscalls 146 and 147.

(146,x%,.2,.2,.7,.7)
(138,x%,.2,.2,.435,.4)
(138,x%,.7,.2,.43,.4)
(138,x%,.2,.9,.43,.4)
(138,x%,.43,.4,.9,.9)

Make up your own lines, or alter these and note the effect. *To alter lines*, use the cursor-lock key to the right of the QWERTY keyboard.

Remember that the second set of values is relative to the first. Experiment with different starting values for x and y so that you can see the effect on the finishing values.

Figure 10.4   The program listing and its output.

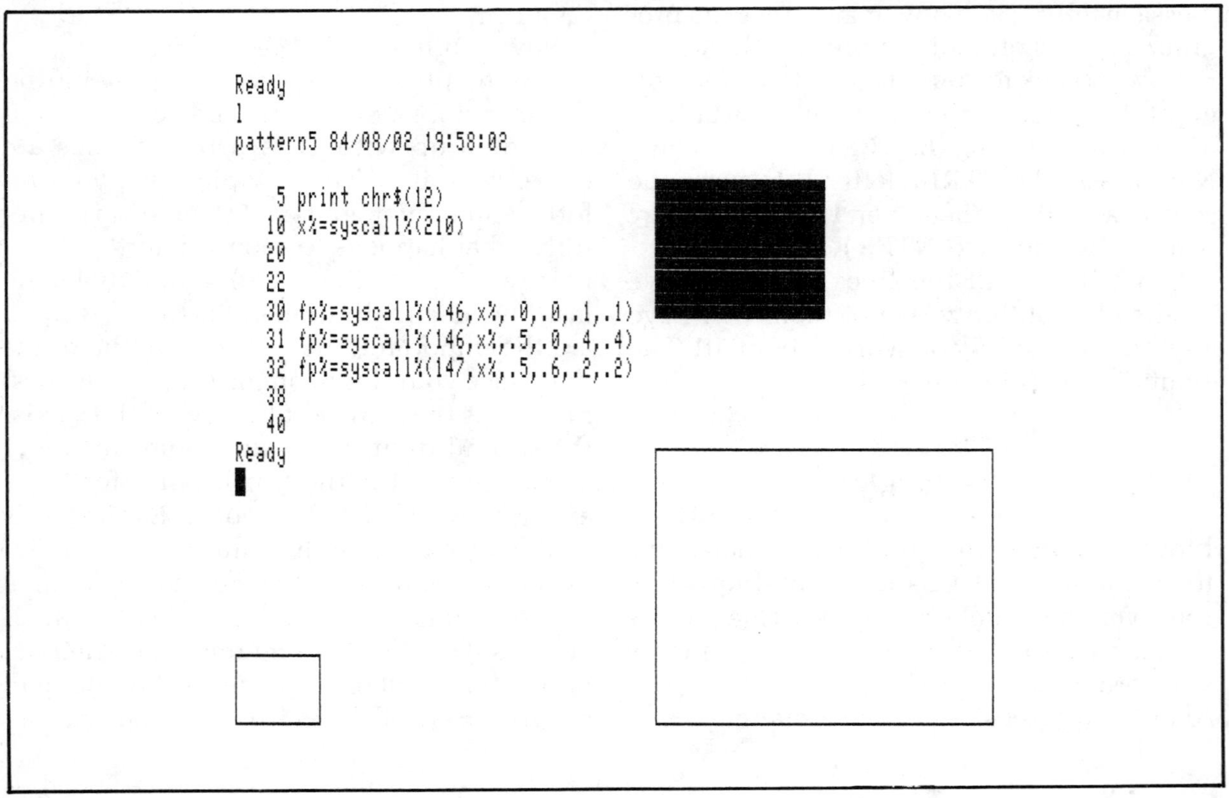

```
Ready
l
pattern5 84/08/02 19:58:02

    5 print chr$(12)
   10 x%=syscall%(210)
   20
   22
   30 fp%=syscall%(146,x%,.0,.0,.1,.1)
   31 fp%=syscall%(146,x%,.5,.0,.4,.4)
   32 fp%=syscall%(147,x%,.5,.6,.2,.2)
   38
   40
Ready
```

Graphics in Motion

It is possible to animate figures on the screen. You have already seen a little bit of that in your earlier programs with nested loops. You can explore it a little more by using the two for-next variables in conjunction with each other, as in figures 10.5 and 10.6. If you nest a pair of for-next loops and then use the variables in conjunction, you can achieve some very interesting effects.

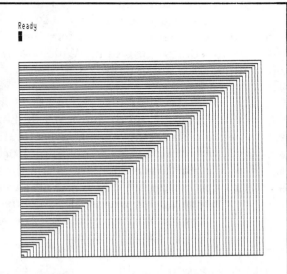

Figure 10.5   Multiple rectangles produced from nested for-next loops.

Figure 10.6   A multiple-line program and its output.

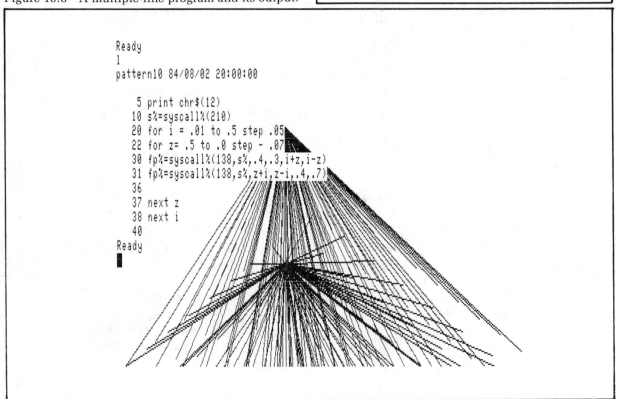

```
Ready
1
pattern10 84/08/02 20:00:00

     5 print chr$(12)
    10 s%=syscall%(210)
    20 for i = .01 to .5 step .05
    22 for z= .5 to .0 step - .07
    30 fp%=syscall%(138,s%,.4,.3,i+z,i-z)
    31 fp%=syscall%(138,s%,z+i,z-i,.4,.7)
    36
    37 next z
    38 next i
    40
Ready
```

Here is a program that you can use and modify to your heart's content. Those of you who are mathematicians can see what you can do with some expressions. Waterloo BASIC supports all the usual ones — SIN, COS, TAN, and so on.

I have used the variable fp% to stand for *filepointer*. Each of the three-digit numbers we have used so far represents a particular activity — creating a line, a rectangle, or a filled rectangle. The instructions for these activities are contained in files. The three-digit number indicates which file is needed. It points your program to the correct file.

```
5 print chr$(12)
10 x% = syscall%(210)
20 for i = .2 to .5 step .1
30 for x = .5 to .3 step − .1
40 fp% = syscall%(138,x%,.1,.1 + i,.5,.5 + x)
50 next x
60 next i
```

STRUCTURED BASIC PROCEDURE DECLARATION

Exploring the possibilities via the syscalls is fun; however, you may find the business of writing endless lines of them quite tedious, particularly when you wish to produce a variety of images in one long program.

Waterloo BASIC, being a structured form of the language, allows you to take short cuts by means of declaring procedures. The principle is the same as that found in Pascal or Forth or C . . . or Logo. If you have played with Logo, you will know that a set of commands can be grouped together, called by a specific name, and then conjured up by the use of that single name. When a teacher ad-dresses a class of students, he or she does not waste time by calling out each individual name; the teacher calls the class by a collective name. The collective name stands for the entire set.

Likewise in Waterloo BASIC. A set of activities can be defined and labeled by a procedure name. Let us look at an example. Say you wish to define a procedure that merely clears the screen.

The CHR$ code for "clear screen" in Waterloo BASIC is CHR$(12). (For Commodore BASIC, it is 147; for Atari, 125; for Microsoft, 26.) A short procedure to clear the screen would look as follows:

```
20200 proc CLEAR_SCREEN
20210 print chr$(12);
20220 endproc
```

Likewise for a graphics procedure:

```
20000 proc GRAPHICS
20010 fp% = syscall%(210)
20020 x% = syscall%(130,fp%,0,0,409,
1365)
20030 endproc
```

A PLOT procedure:

```
20100 proc PLOT(x,y)
20110 x% = syscall%(134,fp%,x,y)
20120 endproc
```

A DRAW procedure:

```
20300 proc DRAW_TO(x,y)
20310 x% = syscall%(136,fp%,x,y)
20320 endproc
```

Now that you have all your procedures in place, you can begin to write the remainder of the program.

```
100 call CLEAR_SCREEN
110 call GRAPHICS
120 call PLOT(0,0.5)
130 call DRAW_TO(1,0.5)
140 call PLOT(.5,1)
150 call DRAW_TO(0.5,0)
199 flag = 0
200 for h = -1 to 1 step 0.01
210 x = (h + 1)/2
220 v = h*h
230 y = (v + 1)/2
240 if flag = 0 then call PLOT(x,y):flag = 1
250 if flag = 1 then call DRAW_TO(x,y)
260 next h
```

This program draws a parabola laid over the x and y axes. The lines 120 to 150 draw the axis lines; the for-next loop draws the parabola.

Save the program with a .bas file name, and then delete lines 120 to 150. Now alter the values in line 20020 as follows:

,20,20,209,1000

The parabola has now shifted down the screen and no longer spreads across the screen. Try changing the first two digits to 100 and see what happens.

ANIMATED PICTURES WITH THE GRAPHICS EDITOR

One of the young people who uses my ICON system was laboriously drawing a series of images with the graphics editor. As soon as he was shown how to use the syscalls, he found a very much faster way of producing the same images. However, for really artistic work, there is nothing to beat the graphics editor.

When you have absorbed enough of the syscalls for the time being, return to the graphics editor; there are one or two things I would like to show you.

Look at Figure 10.7. This image was drawn by my 18-year-old son, Michael. It is actually only a part of an ICONart, the whole thing being an animation. This is how Michael did it.

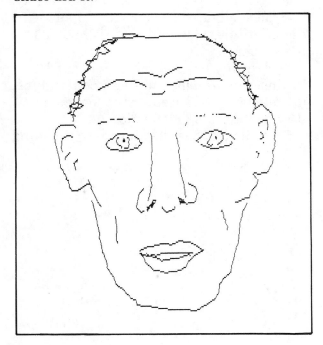

Figure 10.7   A "still" from an animation created with fged.

101

He first drew the outline of a mouth, making sure that the corners of the mouth were well-defined. He then erased all but the corners of the mouth and drew a new version. Alternately drawing and erasing, he produced what amounted to 40 or so "frames", corresponding to frames of a movie film. The result, when displayed, is a moving mouth.

When used in conjunction with the sayer file, which causes the ICON to speak, animation can be very amusing.

You know that the graphics editor has three sizes of letters. The different sizes can be used in conjunction and erased at will, to produce animated signs. The ICON has already been used on television to introduce a program.

SUMMARY

The creation of graphic images using BASIC is achieved by the use of syscalls, which, to be rather simplistic, are utilities offered by the system. In order to access each utility, you must tell the system where to look in the file of utilities. The indicator is known as a filepointer.

Each utility has a number associated with it; thus, for straight lines of a certain type, the number 138 is used; for open rectangles, 146; and for filled rectangles, 147.

Each image has starting and finishing points. The points are designated by numbers, zero/zero (00) being the bottom left corner. The finishing point may be either relative to the starting point or absolute.

Complex images can be created by astute use of for-next loops or similar programming commands available in Watcom BASIC.

Watcom BASIC is a structured language that allows a set of procedures to be identified by one name. A user needs a thorough knowledge of the language in order to produce the most efficient programs.

A QUICK INTRODUCTION TO PASCAL

This book can no more teach you the ins and outs of Pascal than it can teach you everything about BASIC. For either task, a complete text is needed.

The variety of Pascal found on the ICON is that devised at Waterloo University in Ontario, Canada. At the time of writing, the language is designed to be used at Ontario Ministry of Education test sites only. Eventually it will be more widely available. Texts on this variety of Pascal are available, includ-

ing one that is specific to the ICON. I will confine myself to showing you how to use the editor for Waterloo Pascal and how to write a few simple programs.

There is a section on the Pascal editor in the *CEMCORP ICON Training Manual*. In that publication, I give a brief account of the editor and provide a sample program, which I call "waggle". In this book, I will give a more useful program for you to both enter and try to modify for your own purposes.

MAKING A DIRECTORY

It would be wise to make a separate directory for your Pascal programs. Just in case you have not worked with this particular aspect for a while, here are the instructions for creating directories using both the QNX operating system directly and the user interface.

To use the QNX method, give this command:

mkdir pascal

At the return of the shell prompt %, type this command:

cd pascal

Now type this command:

pascal

This stands for Waterloo Pascal.

ENTERING AND SAVING A PROGRAM

When the Pascal language has been loaded from the fileserver, a message will appear at the top of the screen. The rectangular cursor will be sitting under the message.

Press the **⟨ENTER⟩** key.

In the center of the screen will appear two short lines of text as in Figure 11.1 — one of them in reverse mode (black letters on an amber or white block, depending on whether you are using an amber or a color monitor). At the bottom of the screen will appear two more lines: the upper one announcing the language and the lower line indicating what the function keys do when you press them.

Figure 11.1   The Pascal screen before a program has been written.

```
⟨beginning of file⟩
⟨end of file⟩




















█
WATCOM Pascal V2.0 Copyright 1983 Waterloo Computing Systems Limited
```

Type the letter **i** and press **(ENTER)**.

A gap opens between the two lines, ready for your input.

Type in the following program exactly as printed here:

```
program try1(output);
    begin
        writeln('This is my program
        try1');
    end.
```

When you have typed the above, taking the greatest care over the punctuation, type a single period on a new line. The rectangular cursor will now move to the bottom of the screen.

Now type

run

and then press **(ENTER)**.

If you have typed the program correctly, the screen should look like Figure 11.2.

Figure 11.2   A successful Pascal program execution. The program listing is at the top. The command **run** is followed by Pascal's initial statement, the output from the program, the end statement, and execution statistics.

```
program try1(output);
    begin
        writeln ('This is my program try1');
    end.
<end of file>




















run
Execution begins...
This is my program try1

...execution ends
2 statements executed
108 bytes required during execution
                                                    <HOLD>
```

Press **〈ENTER〉** once more, and your program listing will appear with the beginning-of-file pointer highlighted.

The rectangular cursor will sit at the bottom left corner of the screen waiting for your next command, which is this:

put try1

Do not use upper-case letters for this command.

The command **put (filename)** is the equivalent of **save** in BASIC.

MODIFYING THE PROGRAM

Now write a new program by modifying what you already have. To do this, you must use features of the Pascal editor that you have not met before.

Begin by pressing down the cursor-control lock, which is the key marked CUR LOCK just above the HELP key. The small red light will shine, and the cursor controls on the numeric key-pad will be in operation.

Now press function key F9. The beginning-of-file line will no longer be highlighted. Instead, the first character will be highlighted. The highlighting is actually the cursor, which is sitting there waiting for you to move it.

Press the down arrow (numeric key 2) just once. The cursor will obey by moving down to the next line. Move the cursor along the line to the figure 1 in the word **try1**. Change it to a **2** by using the numeral keys on the top row of the QWERTY keyboard.

Press **〈ENTER〉**, and the cursor will move to the next line.

Bring the cursor back up to the line you have just modified, and then press function key F5. A blank line will be created, the remainder of the program moving down. F5 allows for introduction of new lines.

Press the **〈TAB〉** key once, and then enter the following line:

var j: integer

Press **〈ENTER〉** and then F5 once more. A blank line will appear after the word **begin**.

Press the **〈TAB〉** key once, and enter the following line:

for j: = 1 to 10 do

Press **〈ENTER〉** once more, and then press F9. The cursor will move to the bottom of the screen, ready for your next command, which is this:

run〈ENTER〉

The bottom of the screen will show an error message. If you have typed the line **var j: integer** exactly as I asked, the error message should read exactly as in Figure 11.3.

Figure 11.3   An example of an error statement.

```
〈beginning of file〉
program try2(output);
    var j: integer;
    begin

        for j :=1 to 10 do
            writeln ('This is the program called try2');
        end.


program try1(output);
    begin

try2 - Lines transferred = 9
```

Press **(ENTER)**.

The error message will disappear, and the word begin will now be highlighted. Press the up arrow on the numeric key-pad (the CUR LOCK light should be glowing, showing that the cursor controls are now active). The preceding line is now highlighted.

The error message indicated that there was a problem of syntax, and that is so. There should be a semi-colon at the end of this line:

    var j: integer

like this:

    var j: integer;

To insert this punctuation mark, you must first press the letter **i** (for insert). A blank line will appear. Move the cursor back up to the offending line and then along it, using the right-arrow key.

Type a semi-colon and then press function key F9. The cursor will reappear near the bottom of the screen.

It does not matter if the blank line stays in your program. You may type the command **run**, and see the result. If you wish to remove the blank line before running the program, press the down-arrow key on the key-pad; then press function key F6. The blank line will be gone.

The command **run** will let you see the result. Save the program with the **put** command, but call it "try2" this time.

Press **(ENTER)** to return to your program listing, and then modify it once more by changing the second value in the for-do loop.

Write a new line in place of or in addition to the writeln that already exists, making sure that you have the correct format, which is this:

    writeln('statement');

Do not forget the semi-colon at the end of the line!

If you wish to delete a line, bring the cursor to that line and then press F6.

The function keys will also work as cursor controls.

F3 moves the cursor up one line.

F4 moves it down one line.

F2 moves it to the **(end of file)**.

F1 moves it to the **(beginning of file)**.

This may seem to be a lot to remember, and it can be a bother to have to keep on looking for this information in my book or elsewhere. Press F10, and you will see all of the function keys' activities (or functions) displayed. You can press F10 at any time to check on a particular feature. To get back to your program, type a space (press the space bar).

PROVIDING INPUT TO PASCAL PROGRAMS

So far you have developed a program that can only output data to the screen. The following modifications will allow you to input something on which your program can work in order to change the output.

Press F9 to highlight a line. Then move the cursor to the first line, by using either the cursor-control keys on the numeric pad or the function keys. Modify the line by bringing the cursor to the letter o in output. Press the **(INS)** key on the numeric pad. (Remember to have the cursor lock down to do this, or else you will produce just a zero!)

Press the **(INS)** key a total of six times, and then type the word **input** followed by a comma. Your line should now look as follows:

    program try2(input, output);

Now change the 2 in try2 to a 3.

Move the cursor to the next line, and, using the insert (**(INS)**) key once more, modify

107

the line to appear as follows:

    var j,number: integer;

Move the cursor to the line begin, and press F5, inserting a whole blank space. In that space, type the following line:

    writeln('Enter a number between 1 and 20');

Create another blank line immediately after the one you have just written, and in it type the following line:

    readln(number);

Now modify the next line to read as follows:

    for j: = 1 to number do

What you put in the next writeln is up to you.

Put or save the program as try3, and then run it.

Answer the question, and you will see the result.

The next program is a little silly but nevertheless shows how easy it is to manipulate characters in Pascal. There will be a new command that you should, perhaps, explore more deeply in a text on Waterloo Pascal.

The program, including header and tailer lines, will appear as follows:

```
program reverse(input,output);
    const
        border = '*';
    var
        first,second,third :char
    begin
        writeln('Enter 3 characters');
        readln(first,second,third);
        writeln(border,third,
        second,first,border);
    end.
```

When this program is executed, any group of three characters you enter will be printed on the screen in reverse.

Try changing the program to deal with more than three characters; change the constant to some other symbol; change the final readln to produce a different order; or add a couple of lines to produce variations. Use the editing procedures I have described, and save each effort under a different name. Do not forget to change the name of the program, perhaps by adding a numeral after the name ''reverse''.

Now that you have had a taste of Pascal, you may be ready to explore the language further. Be warned, however, that there are a number of varieties of Pascal, and you may find that some programs in books just will not run on the ICON. Either seek the advice of someone familiar with the language or read and practice the instructions in the Watcom manuals.

SUMMARY

Watcom Pascal is available on the ICON and is reached by using the command **pascal**. Currently, Pascal is written using the Pascal editor, similar to the line editor, ed.

Like all other computer languages, Pascal requires that syntax be correct. Syntax errors cause programs to fail.

The function keys play a great part in the Pascal editor. Press F10 to see the effects of all the function keys.

LOGO

HOW LOGO WORKS

It is probable that you have explored Logo at some time or other, or at least heard of this language. It is the supreme computer language of young computerists, used extensively throughout the world to teach small children how to use computers by allowing them to control the activities of an object, called a "turtle", on the screen. The language was originally designed to control a real object —a mechanical, or robot, turtle. Logo is resident on the LEXICON and needs only your command to call it up.

The idea is simple: provide commands that will make the turtle move in various directions. However, the language has a very powerful attribute — one that other structured languages, such as Waterloo BASIC and Pascal, also have. Commands can be clustered together, called by a specific name, and then called by that name in order to execute the several commands. An analogy is in order here.

Consider the following set of instructions:

Stand upright
Lean slightly foward
Raise left foot
Move left foot forward
Place left foot on ground
Place weight of body on left foot
Raise right foot
Move right foot forward
Place right foot on ground
Place weight of body on right foot

Quite obviously, I have given very simplistic instructions in how to walk. The instructions, having once been given, could be provided with a name: "to walk". This is precisely the way the Logo language works, except that the name of the procedure is given first, and then the instructions.

DRAWING WITH THE TURTLE

To call up Logo, simply type this command:

logo

A message will appear telling you that you have successfully accessed the language, and a question mark will sit there waiting for your first Logo command. Type the following commands, one after each question mark (which will appear after you press **(ENTER)**):

fd 30
rt 90
fd 30

You cannot fail to have noticed that the triangular figure moved as you entered each command. You can play with that if you wish, but be careful not to give too high a number after the command, or the turtle will move off the screen! If that should happen, you must try to get it back again.

After the next question mark, type the command (or rather the procedure name, for that is what it really is):

to box

A new symbol will appear: **)**

Type the following, pressing **(ENTER)** after each numbered item. Be sure to type the numbers at the beginning of each line:

1 fd 30
2 rt 90
3 fd 30
4 rt 90
5 fd 30
6 rt 90
7 fd 30
end

The question mark will appear once more, and a message will sit on the screen telling you that "box" has been defined. Notice that the "turtle" has not moved.

Now type this command:

box

Immediately the turtle will move and draw the box, the instructions for which were given in the program.

Experiment with these two commands, but be careful not to try to define "box" again, or else you will receive an error message saying that you have already done that!

Define a triangle, a rectangle, or a polygon, or make the turtle overwrite itself. Produce a random shape.

Another command you might use is **lt**, which stands for "left"; you will already have realized that **fd** stands for "forward" and **rt** stands for "right".

When you have played with these commands for a while, exit from Logo by typing this command:

goodbye

I think you are in for a surprise, for, although I am going to urge you to continue with Logo, the rest of the chapter will deal with a special feature of the ICON — one with which the ICON comes equipped. Logo in French!

LOGO IN FRENCH

The ICON was designed specifically to meet certain Canadian educational requirements. At least 20 percent of the Canadian population speaks French as a first language, and a very large number of English-speaking school children receive all their schooling in the French language.

Even if you do not speak French, you can try your hand at dealing with the computer in French. Why not? You have become familiar with a number of other languages or means of communication, at least at an elementary level: you have explored QNX, BASIC, and Pascal. For all I know, you have experienced a number of dialects of BASIC and have touched a little on Forth, Cobol, and Fortran. Logo in French should hold no terrors.

The command to reach the French Logo is quite simple:

logo.français

When you have pressed **(ENTER)**, the legend **LOGO — Edition Française** will appear on the screen. The question mark indicating readiness for your next command will be waiting, as will the small triangular turtle.

Type the following lines exactly as you see them. The question mark and the **)** signs will appear on the screen automatically, as in the English version.

---

pour carré
1 avance 30
2 droite 90
3 avance 30
4 droite 90
5 avance 30
6 droite 90
7 avance 30
8 droite 90
fin

The message **carré défini** will appear, and a new question mark will sit under it.

Type this:

carré

The turtle will draw a box on the screen.

Now type the following:

---

pour fleur
20 répète 13 [carré ga 35]
25 reculé 50
fin

The square brackets can be found on the QWERTY keyboard, second row down over on the right. They are to the left of the digits 7, 8, and 9 on the key-pad. If you type the line incorrectly, simply start again at the next **)** prompt.

Now press **(CTRL)** and the letter l (∧l) to clear the screen.

Type the word **fleur** after the question mark, and watch the turtle draw a pattern. The pattern, shown in Figure 12.1, is simply the box

repeated 13 times, with each box 35 degrees to the left of the preceding box.

Figure 12.1 Two procedure definitions (carré and fleur), the command **fleur**, and the result of the command's execution.

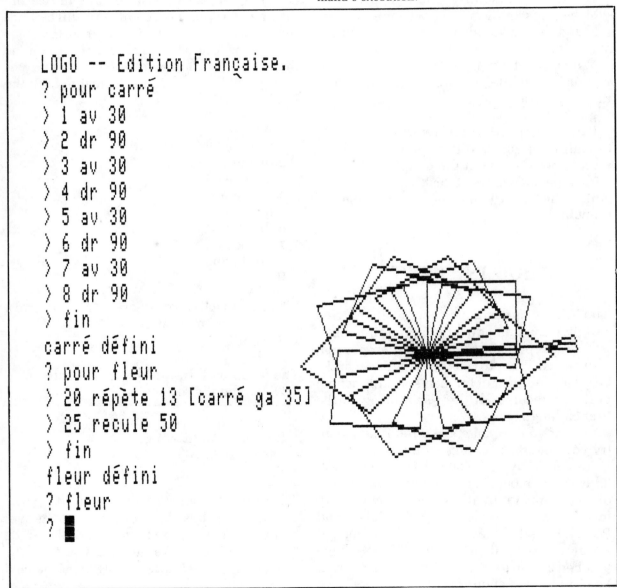

```
LOGO -- Edition Française.
? pour carré
> 1 av 30
> 2 dr 90
> 3 av 30
> 4 dr 90
> 5 av 30
> 6 dr 90
> 7 av 30
> 8 dr 90
> fin
carré défini
? pour fleur
> 20 répète 13 [carré ga 35]
> 25 recule 50
> fin
fleur défini
? fleur
?
```

You have defined "carré", or "box", and then used that definition in a further definition that produces "fleur", or a flower. It could be that you do not think the pattern resembles a flower all that well, in which case you can edit the "fleur" portion by simply typing **pour fleur** once more and changing some of the parameters in line 20. To do so, type this:

pour fleur
20 répète x [carré ga x]

The letter **x** represents the number you wish to place in that spot.

Figure 12.2 The command **fleur** has been issued eight times to produce this pattern.

You can command the turtle to carry out the new procedure several times, examining the result until you see something you like. If you ask the turtle to draw fleur eight times, the result will look something like Figure 12.2. How would you make that into a procedure? By declaring a new procedure and writing a line that calls on the procedure "fleur", like this:

pour fleurs
1 répète 8 fleur
2 fin

You would then issue the command **fleurs**.

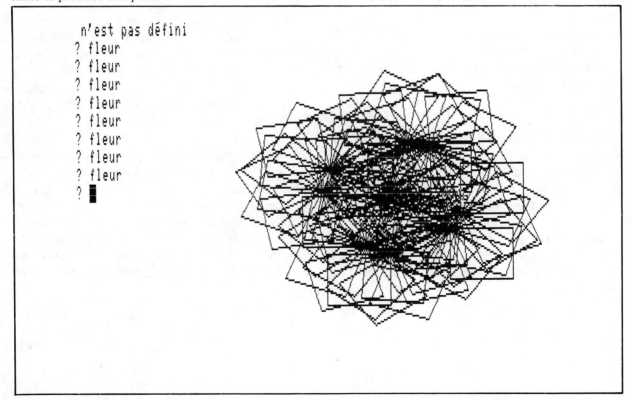

113

Logo permits abbreviations of commands, thus:

---

av = avance = **fd** = forward
dr = droite = **rt** = right
ga = gauche = **lt** = left

Other Logo words include these:

---

répète = repeat
pour = to (to define a procedure)
fin = end (to end a procedure)

Logo does not confine itself to the movement of a turtle and the drawing of lines. The language also supports the presentation of text or the printed word. Consider the following:

---

pour présentation
1 écris [bonjour, comment t'appelles-tu?]
2 écris lisliste
fin

Now type the word **présentation**, and you will see the material contained in the square brackets on line 1 printed on the screen.

There is no question mark—merely a square cursor sitting waiting for you to enter your name.

When you enter the name, the ICON will print it on the screen. The term to use for this printing is *echoing*. The screen echoes what you enter.

You can add to the definition of présentation by typing this command:
pour présentation
Then type the first two lines of the program so far, and input the following:

---

3 écris "enchanté
4 écris lisliste
fin

The **e** on the end of **enchanté** should have an acute accent on it. Use the character to the right of the letter p on the ICON keyboard.

Note that the cursor remains until you either enter another name or just press **(ENTER)**. If you enter another name, the screen will merely echo it without the delightful comment!

If you are going to make extensive use of French, you might make a note of how to produce other accented letters. One example will suffice, for they all work in the same way. If you wish to produce "e" with a circumflex over it (**ê**), type the circumflex first. The cursor will remain in the same spot waiting for you to type the letter "e". If you type the letter first, the ICON will think that you are writing in English and do not require the circumflex.

The Logo language serves as a useful first language and as an introduction to languages such as Pascal and C. Explore Logo in either English or French. A couple of useful texts are listed in the Bibliography at the end of this book.

SUMMARY

Logo is far from being a language exclusively for children or childish programming, although extensive use is made of it in teaching the young about computers.

As in Waterloo BASIC and Pascal, procedures can be defined and called upon to perform complex activities, including both drawing and writing.

The ICON supports a French version of Logo, the commands and error messages being in that (natural) language.

The ICON as an Educational Tool

Computers can play a variety of roles in education. They can facilitate communication: users can set out their thoughts, store them, alter them, combine them, and then pass them on to other users. Computers can clarify thinking: to operate a computer, users must learn to think logically. Computers can be used to drill, to simulate real-life situations requiring decision making, and to administer exams, among other things. The most significant single characteristic of the computer, however, is its ability to provide instruction and experiences that are individualized. Ironically, it is this especially valuable feature that is most at odds with current teaching methods — and thus most likely to prevent full integration of the computer into the educational environment. For students to benefit fully from the ICON's capabilities, the educational system must make some adjustments. In this section, I will offer some guidelines for integrating the ICON into schools.

There are several reasons for the widespread uneasiness among educators about using computers in schools. Fear of the unfamiliar is one; to those who have had no experience with them, computers can seem frightening. Adding to teachers' disquiet are some strange notions about what computers can do. For instance, although word processors can only manipulate text that the student has created, some teachers have the idea that the machine somehow provides the student with an unfair advantage — that using a word processor is cheating. Another fear is that text produced by a printer will be hard to read, as printouts used to be; but printers are improving almost daily — and certainly they produce copy at least as clear as that produced by a student pecking on a typewriter and better than most forms of handwriting!

But the biggest reason for educators' resistance to the computer in education is the change the computer necessitates in teaching methods. Although we know that people acquire and process information at varying rates, schools still attempt to cause information to be acquired in blocks by blocks of people. Teachers' lack of training in individualized methods, and their uncertainty about their role in the computerized classroom, may arouse fears that the computer will make their services obsolete.

In the 1960s, there was an attempt to introduce individualized, machine-based methods of information processing: programmed instruction was the rage. But the method fell out of favor, even though it unquestionably worked. The main reason why programmed instruction did not become a universal method was that imposing a means of individual progress on a system dedicated to the lock-step method produced confusion. The question is, how can we introduce the ICON so that it does not go the way of programmed instruction? The answer is this: by convincing educators of the virtues of individualized instruction, and by making the educational system more flexible.

Teachers need to be given enough training on the ICON to dispel some of their fears. Even more important, they must be reassured that not much formal training is necessary and that a learn-as-you-go approach is both

117

common and appropriate in the field of computers. In addition, teachers should be reassured about the demands of individualized instruction. Yes, it can be more tiring than lecturing, but the range of student abilities in a computerized class will be no greater than in any other class. If "expert" student users are allowed to assist less advanced classmates, the student-teacher ratio will be reduced, and the instructor will be able to give extra attention to the students who need it most.

To make the best use of the ICON, the school system must be flexible in its definition of the role of the computer. The ICON should be incorporated into many aspects of education rather than relegated to the computer lab. High school students are capable of producing short but highly effective learning modules in a variety of subjects — a task that gives students a sense of purpose in their computer studies as well as providing new learning materials. Another way to integrate the computer into school life is to place one or two in the resource center or library.

The school system must also be flexible about scheduling. If the system allowed, the computer could, for instance, administer exams individually, at times appropriate to students' learning speeds, by presenting items randomly selected from a large pool. (Such a program could also be used to pinpoint weaknesses and even present remedial material when necessary.) Ideally, the school day would be organized so that students could work at their computers as long as they wanted to.

I do not mean to suggest that schools should use computers for everything. Like any other teaching medium, the computer should be used only when it is needed. It is a little too early in the computer-use day for anyone to be able to specify exactly when that is. What is important now is that educators be encouraged to experiment. On the basis of their results, they can build educational programs that put the ICON fully at the service of the school.

APPENDIX A
SAMPLE PROGRAMS

SAMPLE PROGRAM I

This program demonstrates the graphics syscalls in BASIC. The program is sectionalized. After typing in the first couple of lines, which include the all-important syscall%(210), you may type in any of the sections, although it might be best to include all of them eventually, just to have a complete example. The syscalls used are 138, 146, and 147.

```
   3 rem box J. HERRIOTT
  10 print chr$(12)
  20 print "First the box "
  30 for d=1 to 1000: next d
1000 x%=syscall%(210)
1005 for i=.01 to .50 step .02
1010 s%=syscall%(146,x%,i,i,i,i)
1011 s%=syscall% (7,x%)
1015 print chr$(12)
1020 next i
1030 print "Now the dot "
1040 for d =1 to 1000: next d
1100 x%=syscall%(210)
1105 for i=.01 to .50 step .02
1110 s%=syscall%(138,x%,i,i,i,i)
1111 s%=syscall% (7,x%)
1115 print chr$(12)
1120 next i
1130 print "Now the rectangle"
1140 for d =1 to 1000: next d
1205 for i=.01 to .50 step .02
1210 s%=syscall%(146,x%,i,i,i+.01,i+0.3)
1211 s%=syscall% (7,x%)
1215 print chr$(12)
1220 next i
1230 print "Now for something completely different!"
1240 for d =1 to 1000: next d
1250 for i =.5 to .01 step -.02
1260 s%=syscall%(146,x%,i,i,i+.01,i+0.3)
1271 s%=syscall% (7,x%)
1275 print chr$(12)
1280 next i
1315 print chr$(12)
1330 print "Now for something completely different!"
1340 for d =1 to 1000: next d
1350 for i =.5 to .01 step -.02
1352 for w =0 to .5 step .03
1365 s%=syscall%(147,x%,i-.03,i-.04,i-.03,i-.04)
1370 s%=syscall%(147,x%,w+.04,w,i+.04,i)
1371 s%=syscall% (7,x%)
1375 print chr$(12)
1377 next w
```

```
1380 next i
1400 print chr$(12),"Hypnotizing isn't it?"
1430 print "Now for something completely different!"
1440 for d =1 to 1000: next d
1450 for i =.5 to .01 step -.02
1465 s%=syscall%(147,x%,i-.03,i-.04,i-.03,i-.04)
1471 s%=syscall% (7,x%)
1475 print chr$(12)
1480 next i
1500 print chr$(12),"Hypnotizing isn't it?"
1510 for i =.5 to .01 step -.02
1525 s%=syscall1%(147,x%,i-.03,i-.04,i-.03,i-.04)
1530 s%=syscall% (7,x%)
1550 next i
1600 x%=syscall%(210)
1625 s%=syscall%(147,x%,.3,.50,.0,.50)
1700 for i = .0 to .5 step .01
1710 s%=syscall%(147,x%,i,.5,.0,.5)
1790 next i
1800 for i = .0 to .5 step .001
1810 s%=syscall%(147,x%,.0,.5,i,.5)
1890 next i
1895 print chr$(12)
1900 for i = .0 to .5 step .001
1910 s%=syscall%(147,x%,.0,i,.5,i)
1990 next i
1995 print chr$(12)
1998 print "147,x%,.0,.0,i,i"
2000 for i = .0 to .5 step .001
2010 s%=syscall%(147,x%,.0,.0,i,i)
2090 next i
2095 print chr$(12)
2098 print "147,x%,i,i,.0,.0"
2100 for i = .5 to .0 step -.001
2110 s%=syscall%(147,x%,i,i,.0,.0)
2190 next i
2198 print "147,x%,i,.0,i,.0"
2200 for i = .5 to .0 step -.001
2210 s%=syscall%(147,x%,i,.0,i,.0)
2290 next i
2298 print "147,x%,.0,i,.0,i"
```

```
2300 for i = .5 to .0 step -.001
2310 s%=syscall%(147,x%,.0,i,.0,i)
2390 next i
2395 print "138,x%,.0,i.0,i"
2399 print chr$(12)
2400 print "138,x%,.5,i,.0,.45"
2405 for i= .0 to .9 step .01
2410 s%=syscall%(138,x%,.5,i,.0,.45)
2420 next i
2430 for d = 1 to 3000:next d
2499 print chr$(12)
2500 print "138,x%,.5,i,.0,.45"
2505 for i= .0 to .9 step .01
2510 s%=syscall%(138,x%,.5,i,.0,.45)
2519 print chr$(12)
2520 next i
2530 for d = 1 to 3000:next d
2599 print chr$(12)
2600 print "138,x%,.5,i,.0,.45   for next loop decremented"
2605 for i= .9 to .0 step -.01
2610 s%=syscall%(138,x%,.5,i,.0,.45)
2620 next i
2630 for d = 1 to 3000:next d
2699 print chr$(12)
2700 print "138,x%,i,.5,.0,.45 decremented loop"
2705 for i= .9 to .0 step -.01
2710 s%=syscall%(138,x%,i,.5,.0,.45)
2720 next i
2730 for d = 1 to 3000:next d
2799 print chr$(12)
2800 print "138,x%,.5,.0,i,.45 decremented loop"
2805 for i= .9 to .0 step -.01
2810 s%=syscall%(138,x%,.5,.0,i,.45)
2820 next i
2830 for d = 1 to 3000:next d
2899 print chr$(12)
2905 for i= .9 to .0 step -.01
2910 s%=syscall%(138,x%,.0,.0,i,.45)
2920 next i
2930 for d = 1 to 3000:next d
2999 print chr$(12)
```

```
3005 for i= .9 to .0 step -.01
3010 s%=syscall%(138,x%,i,.0,.0,.45)
3020 next i
3030 for d = 1 to 3000:next d
3099 print chr$(12)
3105 for i= .9 to .0 step -.01
3110 s%=syscall%(138,x%,i,.0,.45,i)
3120 next i
3130 for d = 1 to 3000:next d
3199 print chr$(12)
3205 for i= .9 to .0 step -.01
3210 s%=syscall%(138,x%,.55,.0,.45,i)
3220 next i
3230 for d = 1 to 3000:next d
3299 print chr$(12)
3305 for i= .9 to .0 step -.01
3310 s%=syscall%(138,x%,.55,i,.45,i)
3320 next i
3330 for d = 1 to 3000:next d
3399 print chr$(12)
3410 s%=syscall%(147,x%,.2,.27,.5,.27)
3420 s=syscall%(147,x%,.2,.05,.4,.7)
3505 for i= .95to .0 step -.01
3510 s%=syscall%(138,x%,i,i+.02,.45,i)
3515 s%=syscall% (7,x%)
3520 next i
3540 s%=syscall% (7,x%)
3599 print chr$(12)
3605 for i= .95to .0 step -.01
3610 s%=syscall%(138,x%,i,i+.09,.45,i)
3615 s%=syscall% (7,x%)
3620 next i
3699 print chr$(12)
3705 for i= .95to .0 step -.01
3710 s%=syscall%(138,x%,i,i+.12,.45,i)
3715 s%=syscall% (7,x%)
3720 next i
3730 for d = 1 to 3000:next d
3799 print chr$(12)
3805 for i= .95to .0 step -.009
3810 s%=syscall%(138,x%,i,i+.12,.45,i+.20)
```

124

```
3815 s%=syscall% (7,x%)
3817 for d= 1to 99: next d
3820 next i
3999 c=0
4000 print chr$(12)
4001 print "Please enter one of the following: 138, 146, 147"
4002 c=c+1
4005 input a
4010 s%=syscall%(a,x%,.3,.6,.3)
4080 s%=syscall%(7,x%)
4090 for d = 1 to 2000: next d
4098 if c<3 then goto 4000
4099 goto 1000
```

SAMPLE PROGRAM II

This short program is designed for young children who have difficulty in writing.

The program prompts the child with the beginnings of a sentence about the cat, dog, or parrot (although only the dog is treated in this version). The child completes each sentence and is finally asked to write a complete sentence of his or her own.

The program is designed for you to complete, modify, expand, or totally rewrite. A possible enhancement might be the ability to print out the story when it is complete.

There is no possibility of editing the story. The child is encouraged to plan the story through for the second time so that there are no errors.

```
 5 rem: story time
 8 dim x$(20)
10 print "Hi! We are going to write a story"
30 print "First of all, choose something from this list:-"
40 print :print "1 CAT,    2 DOG,    3 PARROT"
45 print :print "Enter a number"
50 input a
55 input "What is your name ",a$
```

```
  57 print "Thankyou ",a$
  60 if a = 1 then z$="cat"
  61 if a = 2 then z$="dog"
  62 if a=3 then z$="parrott"
  70 rem :clear screen
1000 print "This is the beginning of our story:-"
1010 print "My name is ";a$;" and I have a "; z$," whose name is....."
1020 input x$(1)
1030 print x$(1);" likes to sleep......"
1040 input x$(2)
1050 print x$(1);" can make two noises. He/she....."
1060 input x$(3)
1070 input " and....",x$(4)
1080 print "I like to .....",x$(1)
1085 input x$(7)
1090 input "His/her fur is very ........",x$(6)
1100 print "Now you write a sentence about ",x$(1)," ",a$
1105 input x$(8)
1110 print :print
1500 print "Here is your story ",a$
1505 for i=1 to 5:print :next i
1510 print "A story about ";x$(1);" by ";a$
1520 for i=1 to 4:print :next i
1530 print "My name is ";a$;" and I have a ",z$," whose name is ",x$(1)
1540 print :print x$(1);" likes to sleep ";x$(2)
1550 print :print x$(1);" can make two noises."
1555 print "He/she ";x$(3);" and ";x$(4)
1560 print "I like to ";x$(7);" ";x$(1)
1570 print "His/her fur is very ";x$(6)
1590 print :print x$(8)
1600 print "Would you like to write another story ";a$;"?"
1601 print :print "Check over your story ";a$;" and make sure that ";
1602 print "names, and words that begin sentences start with a capital letter"
1610 input y$
1620 if y$="Yes" or y$="y" then 10
1625 if y$="No" or y$="n" then goto 2000
1999 goto 4000
2000 print "would you like to print your story ";a$;"?"
2010 if z$="No"or z$="n" then goto 4000
2030 open #3,1pt1:output
2035 print "A story about ";x$(1);" by ";a$
2040 for i=1 to 5:print :next i
2050 print "My name is ";a$;" and I have a dog whose name is ";x$(1)
2060 print :print x$(1);" likes to sleep ";x$(2)
2070 print :print x$(1);" can make two noises."
2080 print "He/she ";x$(3);" and ";x$(4)
2090 print "I like to ";x$(7);" "; x$(4)
2105 input x$(8)
3000 print "His/her fur iis very ";x$(6)
3010 print :print x$(8)
4000 print "Goodbye ";a$
4001 end
8000 print chr$(147)
8010 print "This program is incomplete. It may completed according to your"
```

```
8020 print "own ideas, or the basic idea used for a program of your own."
8030 print "The program is written in a form which is likely to be familiar"
8040 print "to those used to working with machines other than the ICON."
8050 print "Try re-writing it using structured programming techniques."
8060 print :print "Images of a cat, dog, parrot or any other creature you may"
8070 print "wish to include could be prepared using the fged utility"
8080 print " and then merged with your program."
8090 print "I do not advise using the trackball for animal selection as"
8100 print "the program is designed to deal with reading and writing skills."
```

SAMPLE PROGRAM III

Syscalls are also used for tricks other than graphics. In the following programs, the sound chip is brought into play.

There are 63 possible pitches and a sound called ''white noise''. The 63 pitches are not exactly one semitone apart, so the production of melodies can be a trifle difficult, unless you wish to compose music for the sitar or the koto! On the other hand, since the computer is far from being a conventional musical instrument, why should its music sound like that of a piano or harpsichord? As far as I know, there is no way to modify the attack, delay, and sustaining attributes of the sounds. Perhaps you will find a way.

```
 10 rem tone program
 20 print "Enter a number between 1 and 63"
 22 print "Enter -1 to exit from program"
 25 input y%
 27 if y%=-1 then 100
 30 x%=syscall%(216,y%)
 40 for d=1 to 500:next d
 50 x%=syscall(217)
 75 goto 20
100 end


  5 rem tone2
 10 print "Do you know this melody?"
 15 for i = 1 to 16
 20 read y%
 22 for d = 1 to 500:next d
 30 x%=syscall%(216,y%)
 50 next i
 60 x%=syscall(217)
100 data 22,22,16,16,30,30,30,26,22,20,16,13,26,26,26,-1
```

```
  5 rem tone3
 10 print "Do you know this melody?"
 15 for i = 1 to 29
 20 read y%
 22 for d = 1 to 300:next d
 30 x%=syscall%(216,y%)
 50 next i
 60 x%=syscall(217)
100 data 30,30,22,22,30,30,16,16,20,22,22,26,26,30,30
110 data 16,16,13,13,20,20,8,8,10,13,16,16,16,-1
```

APPENDIX B
SAMPLE GRAPHICS

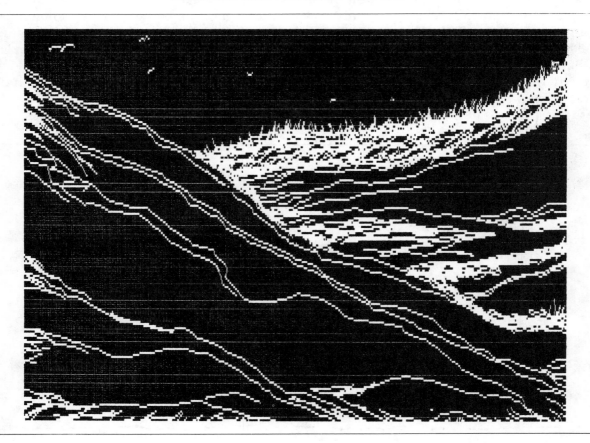

128

Signal Hill, Newfoundland.   DMH'84

BIBLIOGRAPHY

Brown, P.J. *Starting with UNIX*. London: Addison-Wesley, 1984.

Hancock, Les, and Krieger, Morris. *The C Primer*. New York: McGraw-Hill, 1982.

Herriott, John D. "CAI: A Philosophy of Education and a System to Match." *Creative Computing*, April 1982.

Papert, S. *Mindstorms: Children, Computers and Powerful Ideas*. New York: Basic Books, 1980.

Taylor, R. P., ed. *The Computer in the School: Tutor, Tool, Tutee*. New York: Teachers College Press, 1980.

Weidenfield, G.; Mathieu, F.; and Perolat, Y. *LOGO*. Paris: Eyrolles, 1983.

Wright, A. E. *Microcomputers in the Schools: New Directions for British Columbia*. Victoria, B.C.: Ministry of Education, 1980.

QNX COMMANDS

&	send task to the background (option)
basic	access BASIC
cat	concatenate files
cd	change directory to home directory
cd ∧	change directory up one level from current
cd ∧∧	change directory up two levels from current
cd /name	change directory to name
chattr	change attributes and permissions
clearscreen	clear the screen
copy	copy from keyboard input copy from one file to another
date	provide the date and time
dcheck	check integrity of disk
dinit	initialize a disk (followed by drive number)
drel	release (erase) directory
ed	access current line editor
edit	access ICON text editor
[1] fdformat 2	format diskette
files	display contents of directory
files + d	display contents of directory with dates
files + v	display details of files
frel	release (delete) file
hi_res	put screen into 80-column mode
kill	kill a task
list	print a program listing on the parallel printer
locate	find a specified string in a specified file
logo	access Logo (English)
logo.français	access Logo (French)
lo_res	put screen output into 40-column mode

ls	list files and directories	**sort**	alphabetize list or file
mkdir	create a directory	**sprint**	send output to serial printer
natal	access natal language	**task**	list tasks on screen
p	send output to screen	**type**	output text that follows on screen
pascal	access Pascal		
print	send output to parallel printer	**wmi**	indicate current directory and file
query	check status of disk		
slist	print a program listing on the serial printer		

GLOSSARY OF COMMON COMPUTER TERMS

ASCII   American Standard Code for Information Exchange. Each numeral, letter, and other scribal symbol is assigned a number from 0 to 255. Some ASCII code numbers are assigned to screen and printer functions, such as carriage return and clear screen.

Attributes (of a file)   Indicators of relationship between the user and the file; whether the file can be read, written to, or executed by the user.

Backup   The procedure used to provide copies of files from hard to floppy or floppy to hard disk. It is both a precautionary and a housekeeping activity.

Binary system   A counting system based on 2. There are but two symbols (0 and 1), as opposed to the ten symbols (0 to 9) of the common decimal system.

Bit   A single binary number. A "binary digit".

Bug   Its origin is unknown, but the word refers to errors that stop your program from running properly.

Byte   A binary number that has eight bits.

Character   Any symbol that can be reproduced.

Command file   A file consisting of QNX operating-system commands designed to carry out some quasiprogramming activity.

Compiler   A program that works on the code you enter before you are able to run your program. *See also* Interpreter.

Computer-assisted instruction (CAI)   The process (and the software) that causes the computer to act as a tutor. See Computer-assisted learning (CAL).

Computer-assisted learning (CAL)   A term in greater favor than Computer-assisted instruction, denoting the process whereby learning takes place as a result

of interaction with a computer. Any interaction with a computer may be considered a learning process.

Concatenate   The process of sticking two discrete programs or portions of programs together.

Crash   A common computerist term used to describe a terrible state of affairs often caused by a Bug. Sometimes refers to entire system failure.

Cursor   A pointer on the monitor screen that indicates where your input will appear. It can take a number of forms on the ICON. The common form when you are dealing directly with the operating system is a small rectangle. When you are using the text editor, it takes the form of an arrow. The two graphics editors, including ied, use a cross-hair cursor. In certain circumstances, the cursor is not present.

Device   Each part of a computer, whether built in or attached by the user. The screen, hard disk, floppy disk, printer, modem, keyboard, and speaker are all devices, which the computer must treat individually.

Directory   A "super file" containing other files. It is a means of grouping certain types of files and keeping them separate from other types of files.

Diskette   *See* Floppy disk.

Downloading   The act of transferring a language or a file from the fileserver to the ICON work station.

File   A collection of data, be it a program, a set of numbers, a list of items, the coding for graphic images, or a piece of text.

Fileserver   The large flat box named LEXICON. It is

the device that allows for interconnection of several ICONs.

Floppy disk   A flexible, portable disk used for storing computer data in magnetic form.

Floppy disk drive   The mechanism that both contains a floppy disk and records/replays the magnetic messages stored on the disk.

Formatting   The process that divides the disk into sectors in which magnetic data are stored.

General-user account   A means of accessing some of the features of the ICON system without a personal login name and password.

Hard copy   A version of computer output printed on paper rather than printed on the screen or stored in magnetic form on the hard disk or a floppy disk.

Hard disk   A constantly rotating metal disk (or disks) on which data are stored.

Header   An optional statement appearing at the top of each page of hard copy indicating the date and time of printing, the file name, and the page number.

Hexadecimal code   A counting system using base 16.

Hex-pad   A term commonly used to describe the Numeric key-pad. Derived from a now-historic need to enter computer instructions in Hexadecimal code.

ICON   The name of the student station. An icon is a small picture. The ICON system makes extensive use of icons!

ICONET   The name given to the network of LEXICON/ICONS linked together by coaxial cable.

Initialization (of a disk)   The process of readying a disk for acceptance of magnetic data. *See* Formatting.

Interface   A device, physical or conceptual, allowing two otherwise incompatible entities to work together.

Interpreter   A means of translating your program line-by-line into code the computer can understand. An example of an interpreted language is BASIC, although one can find compiled versions of this language too (*see* Compiler). An interpreted language runs slowly.

Key-pad   *See* Numeric key-pad.

Login name   A name typed by the user to gain access to the system.

Multi-tasking   The ability of a computer to perform many tasks at one time, for one user or many.

Numeric key-pad   The subsidiary keyboard to the right of the main QWERTY keyboard. It allows for rapid input of numerical data and doubles as cursor-control device.

Operating system   This is the manager and staff of the computer system. You can deal directly with the operating system, or you can talk to subordinate functions.

Options   Denoted by means of single letters preceded by minus or plus signs, they allow control of the appearance of hard copy.

Output   The result of giving the ICON an instruction or command. The output is to the screen, the printer, the hard disk, the floppy disk, or some other device. The output can be modified by addition of options to the command.

Parallel printer   A device producing hard copy. Messages are passed from computer to printer, and the reverse, in eight-bit units. All eight bits are transmitted at one time.

Password   A special code typed by the user to allow access to the system. The password is known only to the user, the site administrator, and the computer.

Path   The route through the directories and files to the one you want. See Path name.

Path name   The list of directories through which you must pass in order to get where you want to go. A path name for the route London-Singapore might read: London/Zurich/Rome/Beirut/Delhi/Rangoon/Singapore.

Peripheral   An output or input device that can be attached to the computer. An example of an output device is the printer. An example of an input device is the joystick. On some computers, a disk drive is regarded as a peripheral. On the ICON, it is built in.

Port   A name computerists give to a plug or socket of one sort or another. This is where a peripheral might be attached.

Prompt   A symbol appearing on the screen indicating that the computer is ready to accept a command. There are three major types seen on the ICON screen: **$**, which the superuser or site administrator sees; **%**, which the general user sees; and *****, which you will see when using ed. There may be another for the new class of user, other than general or super, being contemplated by the manufacturers.

Serial printer   A device producing hard copy. The bits of data are sent to it one at a time.

Shell   A program that allows you to talk to the operating system. When you type a command, the shell reads it and tells the ICON how to interpret it. You can, if you are an expert, create your own shell commands.

Shell prompt   The percent sign that appears on the screen when you are using the QNX operating system. *See* Prompt.

Site administrator   The person responsible for looking after the ICON system. The site administrator has special operating privileges.

Slaves   Small images that appear at the top of the screen when you are using the icon editor (ied). They slavishly copy the larger icon being created in the center of the screen, to show what the icon will look like when in use.

Spooling   The process of storing a file, which is to be printed, in the fileserver.

Structured BASIC   A form of the BASIC language that allows for the declaration of procedures, which can then be called upon from any point in the program.

System manager   *See* Site administrator.

Task   There are a number of them running on the ICON at any one time—hence the term "multi-tasking". They keep the ICON running.

Terminator   A small plug attached to the ICONET outlets that remain unused. Every system will have two terminators.

Trackball   The small, round, black ball to the right of the keyboard. It allows the user to move a pointer around on the screen.

Utility   A "useful" program already in existence, or written by the user, to carry out frequently needed operations.

Word processing   The acts of writing, editing, formatting, and otherwise manipulating text.

FEATURES OF THE ICON COMPUTING SYSTEM

Processor
Intel iAPX186 high integration, 16 bit microprocessor, upward compatible with the 8086 and 8088
7.2 MHz clock

Local Area Network
A modified ARCNET system
2.5 Mbit/second token passing

Interfaces (optional)
Two serial RS232 ports
Parallel printer port

Diskette Drive (optional)
Half height 640K bytes formatted

Memory
384K bytes RAM expandable to 512K bytes on board and 896K bytes external
Up to 128K bytes ROM
32 bytes EEPROM

Keyboard
98 keys and a space bar in 3 groups: main QWERTY keyboard, numeric key-pad, function keys, trackball.

Video Display
30.48 cm (12 in.) monochrome (640 × 240 pixels × 1 bit)
33.02 cm (13 in.) color (320 × 240 pixels × 2 bits)

Power Requirements
120 V AC, 60 Hz, 250 W

Languages
WATCOM BASIC
WATCOM Pascal
WATCOM COBOL
WATCOM APL
WATCOM FORTRAN
C
Natal
Logo

There are two forms of the ICON work station, which differ as follows:
1. Networking ICON
2. Stand-alone having a subsidiary floppy diskette drive installed in the pedestal.

Work stations can be fitted with either a monochrome (amber) or a full-color monitor.

The Keyboard

Main
Standard QWERTY layout with French characters added.

Further additional keys are
RUBOUT (bottom right) deletes characters to left of cursor position.
HELP (bottom right) provides information on use of numeric key-pad.
CTRL (center left) used in conjunction with keys for special codes.
PAUSE (bottom left) halts scrolling of material on screen.
ESC (top left) used with keys in QNX line editor.

Numeric Key-pad
Normal operation
Numerals
Operators **+** , **−** ,*, **−** .
Enter key
Period and comma

Cursor Lock Engaged
1,2,3 and 5 become cursor controls
7 ⟩ begin line
8 ⟩view
9 ⟩end line
4 ⟩text line begin
6 ⟩text line end
− ⟩end of text
+ ⟩move up one page of text
− ⟩move down one page of text
0 ⟩insert
. ⟩ delete

Function Key Row
ACTION keys at each end function in conjunction with the trackball. Ten numbered function keys may be either preprogrammed by software or, in the ICON editor mode, programmed or mapped by the user.

Trackball: moves small pointer over the screen. Speed of movement may be altered by site administrator or by software producer.

Home clear

Insert and Delete.

ARCNET is a registered trademark of Datapoint Corp.

INDEX